Baltic Sea Crui Guide

Discovering the Beauty of Northern Europe

Margaret Lawson

Disclaimer

The information contained in this book is for informational purposes only. The author has made every effort to ensure accuracy and up-to-date content at the time of publishing, but cruise itineraries, prices, and regulations may change without notice. Readers are encouraged to verify details with the relevant cruise lines, travel agencies, and authorities. The author assumes no responsibility or liability for any errors, omissions, or any outcomes related to the use of this information. Any reliance on the content provided is solely at your own risk.

This book is not affiliated with or endorsed by any cruise line, company, or organization mentioned within. All opinions expressed are those of the author.

Table of Contents

Contents

Introduction

Welcome to the Baltic Sea

Imagine setting sail through a tapestry of history, culture, and natural beauty as you glide across the waters of the Baltic Sea. From the gilded palaces of St. Petersburg to the colorful medieval streets of Tallinn, the Baltic Sea cruise offers an immersive journey through some of the most stunning and culturally rich cities in Northern Europe. Every port tells its own story, every view from your deck is a picture-perfect moment, and every day on board brings new adventures to explore. Welcome to the Baltic Sea— where timeless history meets modern luxury, and every mile is packed with discovery.

Why Choose a Baltic Sea Cruise?

You may be wondering, with so many cruising options available worldwide, why the Baltic Sea? What makes this region such a compelling destination for seasoned travelers and first-time cruisers alike?

The Baltic Sea is a treasure trove of experiences. Unlike the more tropical or temperate destinations where relaxation is the prime focus, a Baltic Sea cruise offers a well-rounded mix of adventure, culture, and relaxation. The diversity of cities and landscapes you'll encounter—from the architectural splendor of St. Petersburg to the charming cobblestone streets of Visby—means that there is always something new to discover.

The Baltic Sea is surrounded by nations that have shaped European history for centuries, and as you cruise from one port to another, you'll find yourself immersed in the rich tapestries of Nordic, Slavic, and Baltic cultures. Every port stop is an opportunity to walk in the footsteps of Vikings, tsars, and medieval traders, with stunning castles, historic landmarks, and modern marvels dotting your path.

Additionally, the Baltic Sea is known for its calm waters and mild temperatures during the cruising season. This makes it an ideal destination for travelers who are concerned about rough seas or extreme weather, ensuring a smooth and enjoyable experience throughout your trip. The region is perfect for those who prefer a more temperate climate, where you can enjoy both sunny days and refreshing breezes without the sweltering heat or biting cold.

But perhaps one of the most compelling reasons to choose a Baltic Sea cruise is the sheer convenience it offers. Instead of planning individual trips to these far-reaching cities, a cruise provides a seamless way to experience multiple countries in one itinerary. No need to worry about visas, long train rides, or navigating foreign airports—your floating hotel will deliver you to the heart of each destination, where you can simply step off the ship and start exploring.

Best Time to Cruise the Baltic Sea

Timing your Baltic Sea cruise is crucial for maximizing your experience. The region's prime cruising season generally runs from late May to early September, when the weather is at its best and the cities are alive with activity.

- **May to June**: Early summer is a wonderful time to visit the Baltic Sea. The days are long, the weather is mild, and the cities are just starting to shake off the winter chill. If you cruise in June, you might get to experience the enchanting "White Nights" in St. Petersburg, where the sun barely sets and the city is bathed in a surreal twilight. The early season is also less crowded, so you can enjoy popular tourist spots without the overwhelming summer crowds.

- July to August: This is the height of the cruising season, with warm temperatures and bustling city squares. It's the best time for those who prefer lively atmospheres and cultural festivals. From music festivals in Riga to outdoor markets in Stockholm, the Baltic cities come alive in the summer months. However, with this increased activity comes larger crowds, especially at popular attractions like the Hermitage Museum in St. Petersburg or the Royal Palace in Copenhagen. Booking shore excursions in advance is highly recommended during these peak months.

- September: For those seeking a quieter, more peaceful experience, late summer and early fall offer an ideal window. The crowds thin out, but the weather remains pleasant, and you'll find the cities starting to prepare for the colder months with a more relaxed, cozy atmosphere. It's a perfect time for picturesque views of the Baltic landscapes as the leaves start to change color, giving you an entirely different perspective of the region's beauty.

Regardless of when you go, the Baltic Sea offers a unique and rewarding experience, each season providing its charm and advantages.

How This Guide Will Make Your Trip Memorable

In the following pages, this guide is designed to not just inform but to elevate your entire cruising experience.

Whether you are a first-time cruiser or a seasoned traveler, this guide is packed with tips, insights, and recommendations to help you make the most of your journey.

- Expert Port Insights: Each port along the Baltic Sea has been carefully researched and explored to provide you with the most up-to-date and comprehensive information. From the must-see landmarks and hidden gems to the best local eateries and shopping spots, we'll ensure you don't miss a thing. Whether you're planning a full-day shore excursion or just a few hours of wandering, you'll find detailed itineraries to suit your needs.

- Onboard Advice: A great cruise isn't just about the destinations—it's about the experience onboard as well. This guide will help you navigate all aspects of ship life, from choosing the perfect cabin to making the most of dining and entertainment options. We'll provide tips on how to book the best spa treatments, what to pack, and even how to handle seasickness should it arise.

- Cultural Context: As you explore the ports of call, you'll also delve into the fascinating history and culture that defines the Baltic Sea region. With background stories about the Vikings, Hanseatic League, Tsarist Russia, and more, this guide will enrich your understanding and appreciation of the places you visit. Instead of just sightseeing, you'll be connecting with the stories behind the landmarks.

- Practical Tips for a Hassle-Free Experience: Worried about visa requirements or how to handle foreign currencies? This guide has you covered. We've included all the practical information you need for smooth sailing, from money-saving tips to health and safety advice. We aim to ensure that your journey is not just memorable but also stress-free.

With this guide in hand, you'll be equipped to make the most of every moment, from the moment you board to the last farewell wave. The Baltic Sea is waiting for you, and together, we'll make it an unforgettable adventure.

Chapter 1

Planning Your Baltic Sea Cruise

Planning a Baltic Sea cruise is an exhilarating experience, offering the perfect blend of history, culture, and natural beauty. However, getting the most out of your adventure requires careful planning and attention to detail. This chapter will walk you through everything you need to know to plan a seamless Baltic cruise, from choosing the right cruise line to booking tips that will ensure you enjoy your trip to the fullest.

Choosing the Right Cruise Line for Your Baltic Adventure

Selecting the right cruise line is the most crucial part of planning your Baltic Sea adventure. Each cruise line offers a distinct experience, catering to various preferences, travel styles, and budgets. Understanding these differences is essential to ensure you pick the perfect match for your journey. Here's a deeper dive into some of the top cruise lines sailing the Baltic Sea.

1. Royal Caribbean International

- **Target Audience:** Families, couples, and travelers who enjoy active and engaging experiences.

- **What to Expect:** Royal Caribbean is one of the most popular choices for Baltic cruises, offering a wide range of activities for all ages. Their ships are known for being massive, filled with entertainment options such as rock-climbing walls, ice skating rinks, and Broadway-style shows.

- **Average Cost:** Fares generally range from $1,200 to $2,500 per person for a 7- to 10-day Baltic cruise, depending on the cabin category and time of year.

- **Example Ship:** Serenade of the Seas – A large vessel offering spacious cabins, excellent dining options, and a variety of activities for families and couples alike. Whether you're zip-lining across the deck or enjoying a formal dinner, this ship combines action with luxury.

- **Website:** http://www.royalcaribbean.com

2. Viking Ocean Cruises

- **Target Audience**: Adults seeking a sophisticated and culturally immersive experience.

- **What to Expect:** Viking Ocean Cruises is designed for adults who want to explore destinations in depth. The focus here is on small-ship luxury, cultural enrichment, and shore excursions that dive deep into the history and culture of each port.

- **Average Cost:** Expect to pay between $4,000 and $8,000 per person for a 12-day Baltic cruise. Viking emphasizes value, as most fares include shore excursions, Wi-Fi, and dining at specialty restaurants.

- **Example Ship:** Viking Jupiter – Known for its Scandinavian design, the ship exudes elegance and comfort. Every cabin has a veranda, and there's an emphasis on cultural enrichment through lectures, onboard performances, and destination-focused dining.

- **Website**: http://www.vikingcruises.com

3. Hurtigruten Expeditions

- **Target Audience: Adventure** seekers and travelers looking for an immersive, eco-friendly experience.

- **What to Expect:** Hurtigruten is known for expedition-style cruising, which focuses on exploration and nature. These cruises are for those who prefer smaller ships, rugged itineraries, and hands-on experiences, like hiking and wildlife spotting.

- **Average Cost:** Typically, $3,500 to $6,500 for an 11-day expedition cruise. This includes excursions such as kayaking, guided hikes, and lectures by onboard experts.

- **Example Ship**: Fram – Designed for polar waters but also operates in the Baltic during select seasons. With scientific experts onboard, guests can engage in educational activities while exploring remote areas of the Baltic region.

- **Website:** http://www.hurtigruten.com

Luxury, Family-Friendly, and Expedition Cruises

Now that you have an overview of the major cruise lines, it's important to understand which type of cruise best suits your needs. Are you traveling as a couple looking for a luxurious getaway? Perhaps you're a family with kids seeking fun and adventure, or maybe you're an explorer at heart who craves off-the-beaten-path experiences. Here's a closer look at the types of cruises available in the Baltic Sea.

Luxury Cruises

For those seeking the ultimate in comfort and pampering, luxury cruises are a top choice. Expect gourmet dining, personal service, and elegantly appointed cabins. These ships often offer a more intimate experience with fewer passengers, which allows for personalized service and attention to detail.

- Example Luxury Lines:

- Seabourn: Known for its ultra-luxury small ships, Seabourn is perfect for those who want an all-inclusive experience. The suites are spacious, and many come with private balconies, offering stunning sea views.

- Regent Seven Seas: Another popular luxury line, Regent Seven Seas, includes all excursions, gratuities, and even shore experiences in the fare. Expect exclusive access to private tours and world-class amenities on board.

- Average Cost: Luxury cruises typically start at around $5,000 per person for a 10-day cruise, and prices can go upwards of $10,000 depending on the length of the trip, cabin choice, and season. While this might seem steep, the value often justifies the price since most inclusions eliminate additional expenses once you're onboard.

- Inclusions: Luxury cruises typically include fine dining, alcohol, shore excursions, and gratuities. Many lines also offer perks like butler service, in-suite dining, and priority boarding.

Family-Friendly Cruises

If you're traveling with children, family-friendly cruise lines offer plenty of activities for all ages. These ships are generally larger and feature everything from water slides and mini-golf to kids' clubs and family-friendly shore excursions.

- Example Family-Friendly Lines:

- **Royal Caribbean**: Their larger ships are ideal for families, offering kid's clubs, family pools, and tons of activities to keep everyone entertained.

- **Disney Cruise Line:** Known for bringing the magic of Disney to the high seas, Disney cruises offer character meet-and-greets, themed dinners, and Broadway-style shows, making it an unforgettable experience for young travelers.

- **Average Cost:** Family-friendly cruises typically range from $1,500 to $4,000 per person, with additional costs for excursions and onboard extras like specialty dining and alcohol for adults.

- **Amenities:** Expect plenty of onboard entertainment, childcare services, and activities for all age groups. Many ships also offer family suites that can accommodate larger groups.

Expedition Cruises

For those who crave adventure, expedition cruises offer the chance to explore remote areas, often with a focus on nature and cultural immersion. These cruises typically feature smaller ships that can navigate narrow waterways, allowing you to visit places larger ships can't reach.

- Example Expedition Lines:

- Hurtigruten Expeditions: These cruises are all about exploration, offering hands-on experiences like hiking, kayaking, and guided tours with experts in marine biology, history, and geology.

- Average Cost: Expect to spend between $3,000 and $7,000 per person for an expedition cruise. This often includes shore excursions, lectures, and the use of equipment for activities like kayaking or snorkeling.

- Unique Features: These cruises often emphasize sustainability and eco-friendly practices, with opportunities to participate in conservation efforts or scientific research.

How to Select the Perfect Itinerary

Choosing the right itinerary for your Baltic Sea cruise is just as important as picking the right cruise line. You'll want to consider the ports of call, the duration of the cruise, and the type of activities that interest you.

Factors to Consider

1. Ports of Call:

- Do you want to focus on the major cities like Stockholm, Helsinki, and St. Petersburg, or are you more interested in smaller, lesser-known ports such as Klaipėda or Visby?

- For history buffs, a stop in Tallinn's medieval Old Town or the Hermitage Museum in St. Petersburg is a must.

- Nature lovers might prefer itineraries that include stops with outdoor activities, such as hiking in Finland or exploring the Curonian Spit in Lithuania.

2. Duration of the Cruise:

- Baltic cruises range from 7 to 14 days. A shorter cruise will give you a taste of the region, while a longer cruise allows for more time to explore each destination.

- If you have limited vacation time, a 7-day itinerary focusing on major cities may be perfect. However, if you want to dive deeper into the culture and history of the region, opt for a 10- to 14-day cruise that visits more ports and spends longer in each location.

3. Example Itineraries:

- **7-Day Itinerary:** Copenhagen → Stockholm → Helsinki → Tallinn → St. Petersburg (overnight) → Return to Copenhagen.

- This itinerary offers a perfect balance of major cities with a mix of culture, history, and natural beauty.

- **14-Day Itinerary:** Copenhagen → Warnemünde (Berlin) → Riga → Klaipėda → Helsinki → St. Petersburg (2 nights) → Tallinn → Return to Copenhagen.

- A longer itinerary allows for more time in each port and includes stops at smaller, off-the-beaten-path destinations.

Exploring Scandinavia, The Baltics, and Beyond

The Baltic Sea cruise gives you the unique opportunity to visit a diverse range of countries and cultures, each with its history, architecture, and charm.

1. Scandinavia:

- Scandinavia is known for its stunning natural beauty, innovative design, and rich Viking history. Popular stops include Copenhagen, with its modern architecture and royal palaces, and Stockholm, often called the "Venice of the North" because of its waterways.

Must-See Attractions: The Little Mermaid statue in Copenhagen, Gamla Stan (Old Town) in Stockholm, and the Viking Ship Museum in Oslo.

2. The Baltics:

- The Baltic states—Estonia, Latvia, and Lithuania—are a delightful mix of medieval towns, stunning Gothic architecture, and Soviet-era history. Tallinn is famous for its fairy-tale Old Town, while Riga is known for its Art Nouveau buildings.

- **Must-See Attractions**: Tallinn's Old Town, Riga's Central Market, and the Hill of Crosses in Lithuania.

3. Beyond:

- Many Baltic cruises also include stops in St. Petersburg, Russia, where you can explore the Hermitage Museum, Peterhof Palace, and the opulent history of the Russian Empire.

What's Included in Your Cruise Fare (And What's Not)

Understanding what's included in your cruise fare is key to avoiding unexpected expenses. Here's what you can typically expect to be included—and what's not.

What's Included:

1. Accommodation: Your cabin, from inside staterooms to luxury suites, is included in the fare.

2. Meals: Most meals are included in the main dining areas, but specialty dining may come with an extra charge.

3. Entertainment: Onboard shows, live music, and most activities are part of the cruise package.

4. Basic Beverages: Coffee, tea, water, and some juices are typically included. Alcohol and soda may cost extra unless you purchase a beverage package.

What's Not Included:

1. Shore Excursions: Excursions range from $50 to $300 per person depending on the destination and activity.

2. Alcohol: Wine and cocktails can range from $10 to $15 each. Beverage packages that include unlimited drinks can cost $50–$90 per day.

3. Gratuities: These are often not included in the fare and range from $12 to $20 per person, per day.

Essential Documents: Passports, Visas, and Vaccinations

Before embarking on your Baltic Sea cruise, ensure you have all necessary travel documents and meet any health requirements.

1. Passports: Your passport should be valid for at least six months beyond the end of your trip.

2. Visas:

- Russia: You will need a visa for St. Petersburg unless you book a shore excursion through your cruise line, which may allow for a visa-free visit.

- **Schengen Visa**: For travelers from outside the EU, a Schengen visa might be necessary to enter certain European countries.

3. Vaccinations: While most Baltic destinations don't have specific vaccination requirements, it's always good to check with your cruise line for any updates, especially in the post-pandemic world.

Booking Tips: When and How to Score the Best Deals

Finally, getting the best deal on your cruise can save you hundreds, if not thousands, of dollars. Here are a few suggestions to help you book smartly:

1. Book Early:

- Many cruise lines offer early-bird discounts if you book 6 to 12 months in advance. This can save you 10–30% off the standard fare.

- Early booking also ensures you get the best choice of cabins, especially if you're looking for something specific, like a family suite or a balcony cabin.

2. Travel During the Shoulder Season:

- Late May or early September is considered the "shoulder season" for Baltic cruises. The weather is still pleasant, but there are fewer crowds, and prices can be lower.

- Example: A 7-day Baltic cruise in May could cost $1,500 per person, while the same cruise in July might cost $2,000 or more.

3. Use Loyalty Programs:

- If you've cruised with a particular line before, sign up for their loyalty program. Many cruise lines offer discounts, free upgrades, or onboard credits for repeat customers.

4. Look for Last-Minute Deals:

-If you can be flexible with your vacation dates, look for last-minute offers. Cruise lines often offer heavily discounted fares for unsold cabins in the weeks leading up to the departure date.

By carefully considering each of these factors, you can plan a Baltic Sea cruise that suits your preferences, schedule, and budget. Whether you're embarking on a luxury getaway, an adventurous expedition, or a family vacation, thoughtful planning will ensure your trip is smooth sailing from start to finish.

Chapter 2

Ports of Call – Unmissable Destinations

The Baltic Sea is a treasure trove of cultural richness, historical grandeur, and architectural marvels, with each port offering something unique to travelers. In this chapter, we'll explore the unmissable destinations you'll encounter on your cruise, from the regal palaces of St. Petersburg to the medieval charm of Tallinn. These ports of call will transport you through centuries of history, while also offering modern delights that make the Baltic one of the most fascinating cruising regions in the world.

Copenhagen, Denmark: The Gateway to the Baltics

As the starting point for many Baltic cruises, Copenhagen is a lively, cosmopolitan city that perfectly blends history with modern flair. Known as the gateway to the Baltics, it's a vibrant, walkable city brimming with royal palaces, fairy-tale architecture, and trendy waterfronts.

What to See: Nyhavn, Tivoli Gardens, and The Little Mermaid

1. Nyhavn

- **Description:** This colorful harbor area, lined with 17th-century townhouses, is one of Copenhagen's most iconic spots. It's a perfect place to take a stroll, enjoy some local food, or take a canal boat tour.

- **Average Cost:** Boat tours typically cost around $15–$25 per person.

- **Tip:** Visit in the early evening to enjoy a drink at one of the outdoor cafés and watch the sunset over the harbor.

 - **Opening Hours**: Always open, with boat tours running daily from 10:00 AM to 8:00 PM.

- **Address:** Nyhavn, 1051 Copenhagen.

- Website: http://www.visitcopenhagen.com

2. Tivoli Gardens

- **Description:** The world's second-oldest amusement park, Tivoli Gardens, is not only a haven for thrill-seekers but also a beautiful garden and cultural hotspot. With live music, theater performances, and over 20 rides, there's something for everyone.

- **Average Cost:** Admission is around $20 per adult, with additional fees for rides.

- **Tip:** Visit in the evening to see the park lit up by thousands of lights—an enchanting experience.

- **Opening Hours**: Daily from 11:00 AM to 11:00 PM (closing at midnight on Fridays and Saturdays).

- **Address:** Vesterbrogade 3, 1630 Copenhagen V.

- Website: http://www.tivoli.dk

3. The Little Mermaid

- Description: This small but iconic statue is one of the most photographed sites in Copenhagen. It's based on Hans Christian Andersen's beloved fairy tale and sits on a rock by the waterside.

- Cost: Free to visit.

- Tip: Visit early in the morning to avoid the crowds, as this spot can get very busy during the day.

- Address: Langelinie Promenade, 2100 Copenhagen.

- Website: http://www.visitcopenhagen.com

Insider Tips for Exploring Copenhagen

- Cycling Culture: Copenhagen is one of the world's most bicycle-friendly cities. Rent a bike for about $15 per day and explore like a local. Most attractions are easily accessible by bike, and the city is crisscrossed by dedicated bike lanes.

- Dining: For a truly Danish culinary experience, head to Noma (4.5 stars), consistently ranked as one of the best restaurants in the world. If you're on a budget, you can also find great street food at Reffen, Copenhagen's sustainable street food market.

- Copenhagen Card: Buy the Copenhagen Card (from $65 for 24 hours) to get free entry to over 80 attractions and unlimited public transport within the city.

Stockholm, Sweden: The Venice of the North

Often called the "Venice of the North," Stockholm is a city of islands, with waterways crisscrossing the capital. It's a stunning mix of modern Scandinavian design and well-preserved medieval architecture.

Must-Visit Attractions: Gamla Stan, Vasa Museum, Royal Palace

1. Gamla Stan (Old Town)

- **Description:** Gamla Stan is one of the largest and best-preserved medieval city centers in Europe. Wander its narrow cobbled streets and admire the brightly colored buildings. It's home to cozy cafés, shops, and several significant landmarks like Storkyrkan (Stockholm Cathedral) and the Nobel Museum.

- **Cost:** Free to walk through, with museum entry fees ranging from $10 to $15.

- **Tip:** Take a guided walking tour for about $20 per person to learn more about the rich history of this area.

- Website: http://www.visitstockholm.com

2. Vasa Museum

- **Description:** This museum houses the Vasa, a 17th-century warship that sank on its maiden voyage and was salvaged almost fully intact in the 20th century. It's one of Sweden's most popular attractions and a must-see for history buffs.

- **Average Cost:** Entry is $15 for adults, and children under 18 are free.

- **Opening Hours:** Daily from 10:00 AM to 5:00 PM.

- **Address:** Galärvarvsvägen 14, 115 21 Stockholm.

- **Website:** http://www.vasamuseet.se

3. Royal Palace (Kungliga Slottet)

- **Description:** One of the largest palaces in Europe, Stockholm's Royal Palace is still the official residence of the Swedish monarch. You can tour its many opulent rooms, see the crown jewels, and witness the changing of the guard.

- **Average Cost:** Entry is around $15 per adult, with discounts for students and seniors.

- **Tip:** Time your visit for the changing of the guard ceremony, which takes place daily at noon.

- **Opening Hours:** Open daily from 10:00 AM to 5:00 PM during the summer (reduced hours in winter).

- **Address:** Slottsbacken 1, 111 30 Stockholm.

- Website: http://www.kungligaslotten.se

Best Ways to Spend a Day in Stockholm

- **Morning:** Start your day in Gamla Stan, wandering the narrow streets and visiting Stockholm Cathedral. Enjoy a fika (Swedish coffee break) at one of the local cafés.

- **Afternoon:** Head to the Vasa Museum for a couple of hours of fascinating history, followed by a visit to the nearby ABBA Museum if you're a fan of the iconic Swedish band.

- **Evening:** End the day with a walk along the waterfront at sunset or take a boat tour of the archipelago, which departs from the city center and costs around $25–$40 per person.

Helsinki, Finland: Design and Nature in Perfect Harmony

Helsinki is a city that marries cutting-edge design with stunning natural landscapes. Known for its innovative architecture, beautiful parks, and proximity to nature, it's a city where you can immerse yourself in both urban culture and the wilderness.

Architectural Wonders and Cultural Hotspots

1. Temppeliaukio Church (Rock Church)

- Description: Carved directly into a rock face, this striking church is one of Helsinki's most famous architectural achievements. Its unique design and impressive acoustics make it a popular spot for concerts.

- Cost: Entry is $4 for adults, free for children under 16.

- Tip: Visit during the afternoon when natural light floods the church, illuminating the copper dome and stone walls.

- Opening Hours: Daily from 10:00 AM to 5:00 PM.

- Address: Lutherinkatu 3, 00100 Helsinki.

- Website: http://www.temppeliaukio.fi

2. Suomenlinna Sea Fortress

- Description: A UNESCO World Heritage Site, Suomenlinna is a sprawling sea fortress built on six islands. It's an easy ferry ride from Helsinki and offers fascinating historical exhibits, walking trails, and picnic spots.

- Cost: Ferry tickets cost about $6 round trip, with entry to most museums on the island costing around $7.

- Tip: Plan for at least 3 hours to explore the fortress and bring a picnic to enjoy the views of the Baltic Sea.

- Opening Hours: The islands are open year-round, with ferries running daily from 6:00 AM to 2:00 AM.

- Website: http://www.suomenlinna.fi

Local Experiences and Day Trips from Helsinki

- **Nuuksio National Park**: Located about 45 minutes from Helsinki by bus, Nuuksio is an ideal day trip for nature lovers. You can hike, kayak, or even stay overnight in a Traditional Finnish cabin. Entry is free, and guided tours start at around $30 per person.

- **Design District Helsinki:** For design enthusiasts, this area is a must-visit. It's filled with boutiques, galleries, and workshops where you can discover the best of Finnish design.

- **Website:** http://www.designdistrict.fi

St. Petersburg, Russia: Imperial Grandeur

St. Petersburg is often considered the crown jewel of Baltic cruise itineraries, and it's easy to see why. With its palatial architecture, vast cultural history, and stunning museums, this city offers a glimpse into the opulence of Imperial Russia.

Hermitage Museum, Peterhof Palace, and the Church of the Savior on Spilled Blood

1. Hermitage Museum

- **Description:** One of the largest and oldest museums in the world, the Hermitage is home to over 3 million pieces of art and historical artifacts. It's housed in the opulent Winter Palace, making it a feast for the eyes even before you step inside.

- **Average Cost:** Entry is around $18 for adults, and children under 18 enter for free.

- **Tip:** Plan for at least half a day here, as the museum is vast. Book a guided tour ($50–$100) to make the most of your visit.

- **Opening Hours:** Tuesday to Sunday from 10:30 AM to 6:00 PM (closed Mondays).

- **Address:** Palace Square, 2, St. Petersburg.

- **Website:** http://www.hermitagemuseum.org

2. Peterhof Palace

- **Description:** Often referred to as the "Russian Versailles," Peterhof is a stunning palace complex with vast gardens and impressive fountains. It's located just outside St. Petersburg and can be reached by hydrofoil in about 30 minutes.

- **Average Cost:** Palace entry is about $15, with additional fees for the gardens. The hydrofoil ride costs around $15 each way.

- **Opening Hours:** Open daily from 10:30 AM to 6:00 PM, with shorter hours in winter.

- **Address:** Razvodnaya Ulitsa, 2, Peterhof, St. Petersburg.

- **Website:** http://www.peterhofmuseum.ru

3. Church of the Savior on Spilled Blood

- **Description:** This iconic Russian Orthodox church is known for its colorful onion domes and intricate mosaics. It was built on the site where Emperor Alexander II was assassinated, hence its dramatic name.

- **Average Cost:** Entry is around $6.

- **Tip:** Visit early in the day to avoid long lines. The interior mosaics are breathtaking, and it's worth taking a guided tour for about $20.

- **Opening Hours:** Daily from 10:30 AM to 6:00 PM.

- **Address:** Griboyedov Canal Embankment, 2B, St. Petersburg.

- **Website:** http://www.spilledblood.ru

How to Make the Most of a Short Stop in St. Petersburg

- **Visa Requirements:** If you're only stopping for a day or two, you may not need a Russian visa if you book your excursions through the cruise line. Make sure to confirm this before you travel.

- Time Management: St. Petersburg is vast, so focus on a few key sites. The Hermitage, Peterhof, and Church of the Savior on Spilled Blood are usually top of the list for first-time visitors.

Tallinn, Estonia: A Step Back in Time

Tallinn's Old Town is one of the best-preserved medieval cities in Europe, making it a popular stop on Baltic cruises. The city's narrow cobbled streets, Gothic architecture, and ancient city walls transport visitors to another era.

Medieval Old Town Charm and Hidden Gems

1. Old Town

- Description: Wander the narrow streets of Old Town, admiring the medieval buildings, town square, and St. Olaf's Church. The city wall, which once encircled the entire city, still stands in parts and can be explored on foot.

- Cost: Free to explore, with small fees for certain attractions like the city wall (about $5).

- Tip: Climb the tower of St. Olaf's Church ($3) for panoramic views of the city.

- Website: http://www.visittallinn.ee

Local Cuisine and Shopping Tips

- **Cuisine:** Try traditional Estonian dishes like verivorst (blood sausage) or karask (barley bread) at restaurants such as Olde Hansa (4.5 stars), where the medieval theme enhances the dining experience.

- **Shopping:** Tallinn is known for its handicrafts. Visit Katariina Käik, a narrow alley where local artisans sell pottery, leather goods, and textiles.

Riga, Latvia: Art Nouveau Heaven

Riga, the capital of Latvia, is known for its extensive collection of Art Nouveau buildings, more than any other city in the world. Its mix of architectural styles, cultural landmarks, and vibrant arts scene make it a must-see on your Baltic cruise.

Discovering Riga's History and Modern Appeal

1. Art Nouveau District

- **Description:** Riga's Art Nouveau district is a feast for architecture lovers. Albert Street is the heart of the district, where every building is adorned with ornate carvings, floral motifs, and whimsical designs.

- **Cost:** Free to explore, with guided tours costing around $20 per person.

- **Tip:** Visit the Riga Art Nouveau Museum ($10), located in a preserved apartment to get a glimpse into life during the Art Nouveau era.

- Website:

Best Places for a Cultural Dive

- **House of the Blackheads:** Originally built in the 14th century, this Gothic-style building was reconstructed after World War II and is now one of Riga's most famous landmarks. Entry is around $6.

- **Latvian National Opera:** If you have time, catch a performance at the National Opera House. Tickets range from $15 to $50, depending on the production.

Klaipėda, Lithuania: Lithuania's Coastal Gem

Klaipėda, Lithuania's third-largest city, is a charming port town that serves as the gateway to the Curonian Spit, a UNESCO World Heritage Site known for its unique dunes and wildlife.

Exploring the Curonian Spit National Park

1. Curonian Spit

- **Description:** This 98-kilometer-long peninsula is a natural wonder, featuring pine forests, dunes, and quaint fishing villages. It's a haven for wildlife and outdoor enthusiasts.

- **Cost:** Entry to the national park is about $5 per person, with additional costs for guided tours and bike rentals.

- Tip: Rent a bike (about $15 for the day) and cycle along the scenic trails that run through the dunes and forests.

- Website: http://www.nerija.lt

Outdoor Adventures and Local Life

- Nature Hikes: The Curonian Spit is crisscrossed with hiking trails that offer stunning views of the dunes and Baltic Sea.

- Local Fishing Villages: Stop by the village of Nida to see traditional wooden houses and visit the Thomas Mann Museum ($3), dedicated to the famous German author who spent his summers here.

Visby, Sweden: Fairytale Island on Gotland

Visby is a beautifully preserved medieval town on the island of Gotland, Sweden. With its ancient city walls, botanical gardens, and charming cobblestone streets, Visby offers a peaceful yet enchanting escape.

Ancient City Walls and Botanical Gardens

1. Visby's City Walls

- Description: The city walls, dating back to the 13th century, still encircle most of Visby and provide a dramatic backdrop to the town. You can walk along sections of the wall and explore the historic towers.

- **Cost:** Free to explore, with some guided tours available for around $10 per person.

- **Website:** http://www.gotland.com

2. Botanical Gardens

- **Description:** The Visby Botanical Garden is a serene spot filled with native and exotic plants. It's a peaceful place to relax after a day of sightseeing.

- **Cost:** Free.

- **Tip:** Visit in late spring or early summer when the flowers are in full bloom.

- **Website:** http://www.botaniska.se

Quiet Escape: Nature and History in Balance

- **Beaches:** Gotland is known for its beautiful beaches, and you can easily find a quiet spot to relax along the coastline.

- **Local Delicacies:** Try saffranspannkaka, a saffron pancake served with berries, at one of the local cafés.

Chapter 3

Onboard Experience – Life at Sea

Cruising the Baltic Sea isn't just about the stunning destinations. While the ports of call are remarkable, the time you spend onboard is equally essential in creating a memorable journey. Whether it's indulging in gourmet dining, enjoying a spa day, or soaking in the entertainment, the onboard experience can be just as rich and fulfilling. This chapter will guide you through choosing the best cabin, savoring onboard dining, and making the most of the wide range of entertainment and relaxation options available to you at sea.

Accommodation Options: Choosing the Best Cabin for You

Selecting the right cabin is one of the most critical decisions when planning your cruise. The cabin you choose will serve as your home away from home for the duration of your voyage, so it's essential to select one that fits your needs, preferences, and budget. The Baltic cruises offer a variety of cabin options, from affordable inside cabins to luxurious suites.

Inside Cabins, Oceanview, Balconies, and Suites Explained

1. Inside Cabins

- **Description:** Inside cabins are the most budget-friendly option, typically without windows or natural light. While they're smaller and more basic, they are perfect for travelers who plan to spend most of their time enjoying the ship's amenities or exploring onshore.

- **Cost:** These cabins range from $1,000 to $1,500 per person for a 7-day Baltic cruise.

- **Amenities:** Inside cabins usually include a bed, small desk, TV, and ensuite bathroom. While compact, they are well-designed to maximize space.

- **Best For:** Budget-conscious travelers, solo adventurers, and those who don't mind a smaller, cozier space.

2. Oceanview Cabins

- **Description:** These cabins feature a window or porthole, offering natural light and views of the sea. While still moderately priced, oceanview cabins provide a more open feel than inside cabins.

- **Cost:** Expect to pay between $1,500 and $2,000 per person for a 7-day Baltic cruise.

- **Amenities:** Along with standard features like a bed and ensuite bathroom, the oceanview cabin allows you to wake up to beautiful views, adding an extra element of enjoyment to your cruise.

- **Best For:** Travelers who want a bit more space and the added benefit of a view without splurging on a balcony.

3. Balcony Cabins

- **Description:** Balcony cabins are highly sought after due to their private outdoor space. You'll have your balcony to relax, read, or sip your morning coffee while watching the waves.

- **Cost:** Prices range from $2,000 to $3,000 per person for a 7-day cruise.

- **Amenities:** In addition to standard cabin features, balcony cabins offer an outdoor sitting area, perfect for catching a breath of fresh sea air whenever you wish.

- **Best For:** Couples seeking a romantic getaway, nature lovers who enjoy the sea breeze, and those who want a touch of luxury.

4. Suites

- **Description:** Suites are the most luxurious accommodations available onboard. They offer more space, premium amenities, and personalized service, including butler service on some ships. Suites typically include separate living and sleeping areas, larger balconies, and upgraded furnishings.

- **Cost:** Prices for suites typically start at $4,000 per person and can exceed $10,000 depending on the size, ship, and length of the cruise.

- **Amenities:** Suites often come with premium perks such as priority boarding, exclusive dining options, access to private lounges, and concierge services.

- **Best For:** Travelers seeking a lavish experience, honeymooners, and those celebrating special occasions who want to elevate their cruise to a five-star experience.

What to Expect from Your Onboard Home

Regardless of which cabin you choose, there are a few universal features to expect in your stateroom:

- **Comfortable Beds:** Most cabins come with high-quality mattresses and plush linens to ensure a restful night's sleep.

- **Private Bathroom:** All cabins feature private bathrooms with showers, basic toiletries, and fresh towels replenished daily by housekeeping staff.

- **Climate Control:** You'll be able to adjust the temperature in your cabin to your comfort level.

- **Room Service:** Many ships offer 24-hour room service (some at no extra charge), allowing you to enjoy a meal or snack in the privacy of your cabin.

Dining Delights: A Taste of the Baltic at Sea

One of the true highlights of any cruise is the dining experience, and Baltic cruises are no exception. From casual buffets to elegant specialty restaurants, the variety and quality of the cuisine onboard will delight even the most discerning palates. You'll have the opportunity to sample local Baltic flavors, international favorites, and gourmet dishes, all without ever leaving the ship.

Cruise Dining Options from Buffets to Specialty Restaurants

1. Buffets

- **Description:** Most cruise ships feature a large buffet that serves breakfast, lunch, and dinner. The buffet offers a wide variety of dishes, including local specialties, salads, seafood, grilled meats, and desserts.

- **Cost:** Buffet dining is typically included in your cruise fare.

- **Tip:** Try to visit the buffet during off-peak times (earlier or later in the mealtime window) to avoid long lines and crowded seating areas.

2. Main Dining Room

- **Description:** The main dining room is the centerpiece of the cruise dining experience. It offers a more formal, sit-down dining experience with multi-course meals. Many ships offer flexible seating options, so you can choose to dine at your preferred time.

- **Cost:** Meals in the main dining room are included in your fare, though some items (like premium wines or certain desserts) may incur additional charges.

- **Tip:** Don't miss the formal nights, when the dining room pulls out all the stops with gourmet dishes and an elegant atmosphere.

3. Specialty Restaurants

- **Description:** For an elevated dining experience, most ships offer specialty restaurants. These venues often feature specific cuisines, such as Italian, French, Asian, or steakhouse fare, and provide a more intimate and luxurious dining environment.

- **Cost:** Specialty dining usually incurs an additional fee, ranging from $25 to $100 per person, depending on the restaurant and ship.

- **Examples:**

- **Jamie's Italian (on Royal Caribbean):** Fresh pasta and classic Italian dishes with a modern twist.

- **Pinnacle Grill (on Holland America):** Premium steak and seafood in a refined setting.

- **Tip:** Make reservations early—especially on formal nights—because specialty restaurants can fill up quickly.

How to Maximize Your Culinary Experience

To truly make the most of the dining options onboard, follow these tips:

- **Try Everything:** Cruise ships offer an incredible variety of cuisine, so don't hesitate to try something new. Many ships include regional dishes inspired by the ports you'll visit.

- **Book Specialty Dining Early:** If you're interested in dining at one of the specialty restaurants, make reservations as soon as possible, especially if you're traveling during peak season.

- **Wine and Beverage Packages:** Many ships offer beverage packages that cover alcohol, soda, and specialty coffees. These packages can be a good value if you plan to enjoy multiple drinks per day, with prices typically ranging from $50 to $80 per day per person.

Entertainment for All Ages

One of the perks of cruising is the sheer variety of onboard entertainment. From Broadway-style shows to trivia nights and kids' clubs, there's something for everyone.

Onboard Shows, Nightlife, and Activities for Kids

1. Broadway-Style Shows

- **Description:** Many large ships feature full-scale production shows that rival the quality of Broadway. These shows are usually included in your cruise fare and run multiple times during the week.

- **Cost:** Free with your cruise fare.

- **Examples:**

- **We Will Rock You (Royal Caribbean):** A musical featuring the hits of Queen.

- **Frozen: A Musical Spectacular (Disney Cruise Line):** A live performance based on Disney's Frozen.

- **Tip:** Arrive early to get a good seat, as these shows can fill up quickly.

2. Nightlife

- **Description:** After dinner, you can enjoy a variety of nighttime activities, including live music, karaoke, comedy shows, and dancing at the nightclub.

- **Cost:** Most nightlife options are free, but drinks in bars and lounges typically cost between $8 and $15 per drink.

- **Tip:** Check the daily itinerary (usually delivered to your cabin) to see the schedule of events and performances each evening.

3. Kids' Clubs

- **Description:** Most cruise ships offer kids' clubs for various age groups, with supervised activities like arts and crafts, video games, movie nights, and scavenger hunts. These clubs allow parents to enjoy some time alone while the kids have fun in a safe environment.

- **Cost:** Generally free, though some ships may charge for late-night group babysitting.

- **Examples:**

- **Adventure Ocean (Royal Caribbean):** Activities for kids ages 3 to 17, with different programs for different age groups.

- **Oceaneer Club (Disney Cruise Line):** ThemedRooms and activities are themed around Disney characters and movies.

- **Tip:** Make sure to register your kids for the club on the first day to ensure they get a spot.

How to Stay Entertained Between Ports

On sea days, you'll want to make the most of the onboard amenities. Here are a few ideas that will keep you entertained:

- **Pools and Water Slides:** Many ships have multiple pools and water slides to enjoy during the day.

- **Mini-Golf, Rock Climbing, and Zip Lines:** For adventure seekers, some ships offer mini-golf courses, rock climbing walls, and even zip lines.

- **Trivia and Game Shows: If** you prefer a more laid-back activity, try participating in a trivia game or game show—prizes are often offered for the winners.

Wellness and Relaxation at Sea

Your cruise isn't just about fun and food—it's also the perfect opportunity to relax and rejuvenate. Many ships feature top-notch spa facilities, fitness centers, and wellness programs to help you unwind.

Spa Treatments, Fitness Centers, and Mindfulness Programs

1. Spa Treatments

- **Description:** Most cruise ships offer a range of spa treatments, including massages, facials, body scrubs, and beauty treatments. Some ships even offer thermal rooms and hydrotherapy pools.

- **Cost:** Treatments range from $100 to $250, depending on the service.

- **Examples:**

- **Mandara Spa (Norwegian Cruise Line):** Offers a full range of treatments, including hot stone massages and couples' treatments.

- **Canyon Ranch Spa (Celebrity Cruises):** Known for its luxurious treatments and health-focused services.

- **Tip:** Look out for spa specials on sea days, when discounts are often offered.

2. Fitness Centers

- **Description:** If you like to stay active, most ships have fully equipped fitness centers with treadmills, weights, and fitness classes like yoga and spin.

- **Cost:** Access to the gym is usually free, though some specialty classes may incur a fee (usually around $10–$15 per class).

- **Tip**: Go early in the morning to avoid the crowds, especially on sea days.

3. Mindfulness and Wellness Programs

- **Description:** Many cruise lines now offer wellness programs that include mindfulness classes, meditation, and yoga. These programs help passengers relax and de-stress.

- **Cost:** Wellness classes are typically free, though some more specialized classes (like aerial yoga) may cost $15–$25.

- **Examples:**

- **Princess Cruises' Lotus Spa:** Offers a range of wellness programs, including guided meditation and detox treatments.

- **Celebrity Cruises' "Women in Wellness" program:** Features classes designed by female wellness experts, focusing on mindfulness and self-care.

Pampering Yourself in the Baltic Breeze

If your cruise is a special occasion or you simply want to indulge in some pampering, consider booking a private cabana or VIP spa day. Many ships offer exclusive areas with private hot tubs, loungers, and personal attendants.

- **Cost:** Cabanas and private spa experiences can cost anywhere from $200 to $500 per day.

- **Tip:** Book these experiences as early as possible, as they tend to sell out quickly.

Insider's Guide to Onboard Etiquette

Cruising has its own set of unwritten rules and etiquette, especially when it comes to formal nights, dress codes, and interactions with fellow passengers.

Navigating Formal Nights and Dress Codes

1. Formal Nights

- **Description:** Most cruise lines have one or two formal nights during the cruise, where passengers are encouraged to dress up for dinner and the evening's entertainment.

- **Dress Code: For** men, formal wear typically includes a suit or tuxedo, while women wear evening gowns or cocktail dresses.

- **Tip:** While participation is optional, formal nights offer a fun chance to dress up and enjoy a more glamorous dining experience.

2. Casual Days

- **Description:** On most days, the dress code is casual. During the day, comfortable clothing like shorts, t-shirts, and swimwear is acceptable. In the evening, "smart casual" attire is usually recommended, meaning no shorts, flip-flops, or tank tops.

- **Tip:** Pack a variety of outfits to suit different occasions, and bring a light jacket or shawl for cooler evenings.

Chapter 4

Shore Excursions – Making the Most of Each Port

The excitement of any Baltic Sea cruise extends beyond life onboard to the myriad of experiences waiting at each port of call. From the palatial wonders of St. Petersburg to the pristine landscapes of Finland, shore excursions give you the chance to dive deeper into the culture, history, and beauty of each destination. However, to maximize these experiences, you'll need to decide whether to book cruise-organized excursions or venture out on your own. In this chapter, we'll explore all the ways you can make the most of each port, from the best shore excursions to tips for independent exploration.

Booking Shore Excursions vs. Exploring Independently

When your ship docks in each Baltic port, you'll be faced with a choice: Should you book a shore excursion through the cruise line or explore independently? Both options come with their pros and cons, and the right choice often depends on your travel style, budget, and what you want to get out of the experience.

Cruise-Organized Shore Excursions

Shore excursions booked through your cruise line are designed to make your visit to each port as convenient and stress-free as possible. These are often guided tours that focus on key attractions, local culture, or outdoor activities.

- **Cost:** Prices vary depending on the type of tour, but generally range from $50 to $300 per person, depending on the destination and the activity. For example, a guided tour of the Hermitage Museum in St. Petersburg might cost around $120 per person, while a full-day excursion to Peterhof Palace and its gardens could be closer to $200.

- **What's Included:** Cruise-organized excursions typically include transportation to and from the ship, admission fees, and the services of a local guide. Some excursions also include meals or refreshments.

- **Peace of Mind:** One major benefit of booking through your cruise line is that the ship will wait for you if your tour is delayed. This eliminates the stress of returning to the ship on time and allows you to focus on enjoying your day.

Exploring Independently

For the more adventurous traveler, exploring a port on your own can be a more flexible and often less expensive option. Many Baltic cities have well-connected public transportation systems and are easily navigable on foot, making it easy to explore at your own pace.

- **Cost:** Independent exploration is often cheaper. For instance, a DIY day in Tallinn might cost around $25 for entry to key sites like the city wall and St. Olaf's Church, whereas a guided cruise excursion could be $80 to $100.

- **Freedom and Flexibility**: You can set your schedule, skip crowded tourist spots, and spend more time in places that interest you. You can also choose to dine in local restaurants instead of sticking with a pre-planned itinerary.

- **Challenges:** The downside is that you'll need to be mindful of time, as the ship won't wait if you're late. You'll also need to handle logistics such as transportation, entry fees, and directions, which can be tricky if you're unfamiliar with the language or local customs.

Pros and Cons of Cruise Line Excursions

Understanding the advantages and drawbacks of booking excursions through the cruise line is key to making an informed decision.

Pros

1. Convenience: Everything is arranged for you, from transportation to tickets, allowing you to relax and enjoy the experience.

2. Expert Guides: Cruise excursions typically include a knowledgeable local guide who can offer insights into the history, culture, and hidden gems of each destination.

3. Guaranteed Return to Ship: If your excursion runs late, the ship will wait for you, ensuring you don't miss your departure.

Cons

1. Higher Costs: Cruise-organized tours are usually more expensive than doing it on your own. While you're paying for convenience, the markup can be significant.

2. Crowds: Cruise excursions often involve large groups, which can make certain experiences feel rushed or impersonal. You might not have the flexibility to linger at places you enjoy.

3. Limited Customization: With a pre-set itinerary, you may miss out on seeing something off the beaten path or spending more time in a place that captures your interest.

Tips for DIY Exploration in Each Port

For those who prefer to venture out independently, here are some key tips to help you maximize your day in each Baltic port.

1. Research in Advance: Before your cruise, research each port to identify the must-see attractions, local eateries, and transportation options. For example, in Stockholm, you can purchase a SL Travelcard (about $14 for a 24-hour pass), which gives you unlimited access to buses, trams, and ferries.

2. Use Local Transport: Most Baltic cities have excellent public transport systems. Helsinki, for instance, offers a day pass for around $10 that includes unlimited travel on trams, buses, and ferries, making it easy to visit Suomenlinna or the Rock Church on your own.

3. Start Early: Independent exploration gives you the freedom to beat the crowds. Try to disembark early to enjoy popular sites like Nyhavn in Copenhagen or Gamla Stan in Stockholm before they fill up with other tourists.

4. Plan Your Return: Always leave extra time to return to the ship. Aim to be back at least an hour before the all-aboard time to avoid any mishaps. Use apps like Google Maps for public transit routes or download offline maps of the area to help you navigate.

Top Baltic Sea Excursions for Culture and Adventure

Baltic ports offer a rich variety of shore excursions that cater to every type of traveler, from history buffs to adventure seekers. Here are some of the top excursions you won't want to miss:

1. St. Petersburg, Russia – Hermitage Museum and Peterhof Palace

- Description: These two iconic attractions are among the most popular in St. Petersburg. The Hermitage Museum houses one of the world's greatest art collections, while Peterhof Palace, with its stunning fountains and gardens, is known as the "Russian Versailles."

- Cost: A full-day guided tour combining both attractions costs around $200 per person.

- Tip: Opt for a smaller group tour to avoid the rush and enjoy a more personalized experience.

- Website: http://www.hermitagemuseum.org

2. Tallinn, Estonia – Medieval Old Town and City Wall Walk

- **Description:** Tallinn's Old Town is a UNESCO World Heritage Site, renowned for its preserved medieval architecture. A guided walking tour will take you through cobblestone streets, past Gothic churches, and along the ancient city walls.

- **Cost:** Guided tours start at around $50 per person, while entry to the city wall costs about $5.

- **Tip:** You can easily explore Old Town on your own for free, but consider paying for a guide if you're interested in learning more about the city's rich history.

- **Website:** http://www.visittallinn.ee

3. Riga, Latvia – Art Nouveau District and Central Market

- **Description:** Riga is famous for its Art Nouveau architecture, and a guided tour of the district will introduce you to the intricate designs and history of this stunning style. Afterward, visit the Central Market, housed in old zeppelin hangars, where you can sample local delicacies.

- **Cost:** Tours start at $40 per person, and entry to the Art Nouveau Museum is about $10.

- **Tip:** The Central Market is free to enter, so even if you skip the guided tour, you can still enjoy this vibrant local experience.

- **Website:** http://www.rigamuseum.lv

Best Day Trips from Each Port of Call

If you want to explore beyond the immediate vicinity of each port, many cities offer fantastic day trips that allow you to experience more of the region.

1. Copenhagen to Kronborg Castle

- **Description:** Known as the setting for Shakespeare's Hamlet, Kronborg Castle is a UNESCO World Heritage Site located in the town of Helsingør, about an hour from Copenhagen.

- **Cost:** Entry to the castle is about $18, and a round-trip train ticket from Copenhagen costs around $15.

- **Tip:** Combine a visit to Kronborg with a stop at the nearby Louisiana Museum of Modern Art, one of Denmark's top cultural attractions.

- **Website:** http://www.kronborg.dk

2. Stockholm to Drottningholm Palace

- **Description:** A short boat ride from Stockholm takes you to Drottningholm Palace, the private residence of the Swedish royal family and a UNESCO World Heritage Site.

- **Cost:** A boat trip and palace entry combo ticket costs around $35 per person.

- **Tip:** Time your visit to watch the Royal Guards' parade or attend a performance at the palace's historic theater.

- **Website**: http://www.kungligaslotten.se

Active Adventures: Hiking, Biking, and Water Sports in the Baltics

For those who crave outdoor adventure, the Baltic region is filled with opportunities to explore nature beyond the city limits.

1. Hiking in Nuuksio National Park, Finland

- **Description:** Just 45 minutes from Helsinki, Nuuksio National Park offers beautiful hiking trails through forests, lakes, and rocky outcrops. You can spend the day hiking, canoeing, or even swimming in the park's pristine waters.

- **Cost:** Entry to the park is free, though guided hikes cost around $30 per person.

- **Website:** http://www.nationalparks.fi

2. Biking in Copenhagen, Denmark

- **Description:** Copenhagen is one of the most bike-friendly cities in the world. Rent a bike (around $15 per day) and explore the city at your own pace. For a longer ride, head to the countryside to explore quaint villages and coastal views.

- **Tip:** Be sure to check out the scenic bike route along the water from Copenhagen to the beach town of Amager Strandpark.

- **Website:** http://www.visitcopenhagen.com

3. Kayaking in the Stockholm Archipelago, Sweden

- **Description:** The Stockholm Archipelago is made up of thousands of islands, many of which are best explored by kayak. Guided kayak tours take you through the tranquil waters, offering stunning views and opportunities to see local wildlife.

- **Cost:** Kayak rentals start at $25 per hour, with guided tours costing around $70 for a half-day adventure.

- **Website:** http://www.stockholmarchipelago.se

Where to Experience Nature Beyond the Ship

For nature lovers, the Baltic region is full of scenic spots where you can immerse yourself in pristine landscapes.

1. Curonian Spit, Lithuania

- **Description:** The Curonian Spit is a 98-kilometer-long dune peninsula shared by Lithuania and Russia. It's a UNESCO World Heritage Site and offers unique landscapes, wildlife, and picturesque fishing villages.

- **Cost:** Entry to the national park is about $5, with additional costs for guided tours.

- **Tip:** Rent a bike in Klaipėda and cycle along the Curonian Spit for an unforgettable day of nature and exploration.

- **Website:** http://www.nerija.lt

Cultural Immersion: Local Tours with a Personal Touch

If you're looking to dive deeper into the local culture, consider booking a private or small-group tour that focuses on local traditions and customs.

1. Cooking Classes in St. Petersburg

- **Description:** Learn how to make traditional Russian dishes, such as borscht and pelmeni, during a hands-on cooking class. These intimate classes often take place in the home of a local chef, giving you an authentic taste of Russian hospitality.

- **Cost**: Classes typically cost around $80 to $100 per person and include a meal.

- **Tip:** Pair your cooking class with a local market tour to learn about traditional ingredients and flavors.

- **Website:** http://www.foodandfun.com

2. Folk Traditions in Estonia

- **Description:** In Tallinn, you can participate in workshops that focus on traditional Estonian crafts, such as weaving, embroidery, and pottery. These workshops are a great way to connect with local artisans and learn more about Estonian folk culture.

- **Cost:** Workshops range from $30 to $60 per person, depending on the craft.

- **Website:** http://www.visittallinn.ee

Responsible Tourism: How to Be a Respectful Traveler

As a responsible traveler, it's essential to respect the local culture, environment, and communities you visit. Here are a few tips to ensure you travel responsibly:

1. Support Local Businesses: When shopping or dining in port, opt for locally owned establishments. This helps support the local economy and ensures that your money stays within the community.

2. Reduce Plastic Waste: Bring a reusable water bottle and shopping bag to minimize single-use plastics. Many Baltic ports have refill stations, so you can easily stay hydrated without buying plastic bottles.

3. Respect Cultural Sites: Be mindful of local customs and rules when visiting religious or historical sites. Dress appropriately, avoid touching artifacts, and always follow the guidance of your tour leader or site staff.

Chapter 5

Baltic Sea Cruise Packing List

Embarking on a Baltic Sea cruise offers an incredible opportunity to explore some of the most historically rich, naturally beautiful, and culturally diverse cities in Northern Europe. However, with its ever-changing weather and the varied nature of activities both on and off the ship, packing the right items can be a challenge. From ensuring you have the right gear for the Baltic climate to remembering the must-have cruise essentials, this guide will help you prepare for your journey, so you can enjoy every second of your journey.

Packing for the Baltic Climate: What to Bring for Every Season

The weather in the Baltic region can be unpredictable, with fluctuations from cool to warm temperatures, even during the summer months. Preparing for these changes in advance ensures you're ready for anything, whether you're walking the cobblestone streets of Tallinn, enjoying the gardens of Peterhof, or strolling along the waterfront in Helsinki.

Spring (April–June)

In the early months of the cruise season, expect chilly mornings and evenings, with daytime highs ranging from 45°F to 60°F (7°C to 15°C). Rain showers are also common, so layering and waterproof gear are essential.

- What to Pack:

- Lightweight Layers: Bring a mix of long-sleeve shirts, sweaters, and a waterproof jacket for layering. A packable down jacket is a good option because it provides warmth without taking up much space in your luggage.

- Waterproof Footwear: Choose comfortable, waterproof walking shoes, especially for city explorations. Prices for quality waterproof shoes range from $80 to $150 depending on the brand. Consider brands like Merrell or Columbia for durable and weather-resistant footwear.

- Compact Umbrella: A small travel umbrella (around $10 to $20) can be a lifesaver on rainy days.

Summer (June–August)

Summer is the most popular time for Baltic cruises, with daytime temperatures typically ranging between 60°F and 75°F (16°C to 24°C). However, it's not uncommon to experience cooler days, especially in coastal areas, so having versatile layers is still important.

- What to Pack:

- Light Jackets and Cardigans: Even though summer can be warm, the evenings can be quite cool. Pack light jackets or cardigans to layer over short sleeves when needed.

- Comfortable Walking Shoes: You'll be walking a lot while exploring ports like Stockholm and Copenhagen, so bring breathable but sturdy shoes. Look for options like Skechers Go Walk or Nike Free RN, which retail for $50 to $100.

- **Sunglasses and Hat**: The Baltic region enjoys long daylight hours in the summer, so bring sunglasses (polarized options like Ray-Bans range from $100 to $200) and a sunhat to protect yourself from the bright sun.

Fall (September–October)

Autumn in the Baltics brings cooler temperatures and the possibility of rain, with daytime highs ranging between 50°F and 60°F (10°C to 15°C). Layers are essential, as are waterproof items.

- **What to Pack:**

- **Insulated Outerwear:** A lightweight insulated jacket (costing between $50 and $150) is essential for the cooler weather.

- **Waterproof Pants:** If you plan to do a lot of walking or hiking, waterproof pants or jeans with a water-resistant coating will keep you dry and comfortable.

- Scarves and Gloves: **The wind can be biting in the fall,** especially near the coast, so pack a warm scarf and gloves (typically priced at $20 to $40).

Winter (November–March)

Although Baltic cruises are rare in winter due to the cold weather and shorter daylight hours, some specialized holiday cruises do take place. Expect temperatures to hover around freezing, and snow is a possibility.

- What to Pack:

- Heavy Coat: A winter coat that's both insulated and windproof (such as a North Face or Patagonia jacket, typically costing $150 to $300) will keep you warm while sightseeing.

- Thermal Layers: Pack thermal tops and bottoms to wear underneath your clothes. Brands like Uniqlo or Heattech sell these for about $20 to $50 per piece.

- Waterproof Boots: Invest in insulated, waterproof boots to keep your feet warm and dry in snowy or icy conditions. Boots from brands like Sorel or Timberland cost between $100 and $200.

Cruise Essentials You Can't Forget

Beyond clothing, several must-have items will ensure you have a smooth and enjoyable cruise experience.

1. Power Strip or USB Charger

- Description: Cruise ship cabins often have limited electrical outlets. Bringing a power strip (one that's cruise-approved) or a multi-port USB charger can help you keep all your devices powered. Expect to pay between $20 and $30 for a good-quality surge protector with USB ports.

- **Tip:** Make sure the power strip doesn't have a surge protector, as most cruise lines don't allow them due to fire hazards.

2. Refillable Water Bottle

- **Description:** Staying hydrated is essential, especially when you're exploring ports on foot. A refillable water bottle, like a Hydro Flask or Nalgene (costing $20 to $40), will help you avoid buying single-use plastic bottles during your trip.

- **Tip:** Check whether your ship offers water stations where you can refill your bottle for free.

3. Motion Sickness Remedies

- **Description:** Even if you don't normally get seasick, the Baltic Sea can sometimes be choppy. Pack motion sickness remedies like Dramamine (about $10) or Sea-Bands (around $15) just in case.

4. Daypack

- **Description:** A lightweight daypack or crossbody bag (typically $30 to $60) is essential for carrying your camera, wallet, water bottle, and other necessities when you head ashore for excursions.

- **Tip:** Look for bags with anti-theft features, such as lockable zippers or RFID-blocking technology.

5. Sunscreen

- **Description:** The long summer days in the Baltics can lead to more sun exposure than you might expect. Bring a high-SPF sunscreen (30 or higher) to protect your skin. Prices for quality sunscreen range from $10 to $20.

Important Travel Documents and Electronics

Cruises require a unique set of travel documents and electronics to keep things running smoothly, and it's crucial to pack these in advance.

1. Passport and Visas

- **Description:** A valid passport is essential for any international cruise. Make sure your passport is valid for at least six months after your return date. If your cruise stops in Russia (e.g., St. Petersburg), check if you need a visa. Most travelers on cruise-organized shore excursions don't need individual visas, but those exploring independently will likely need to apply in advance. Russian visas can cost up to $160, depending on your nationality.

- **Tip:** Keep copies of your passport (both physical and digital) in case you lose the original while traveling.

2. Travel Insurance

- **Description:** Travel insurance is essential for covering medical emergencies, trip cancellations, and lost luggage. Plans typically cost around 4-10% of your trip's total cost. Popular providers include Allianz and Travel Guard.

- **Tip:** Be sure to choose a plan that includes cruise coverage and emergency medical evacuation.

3. Cell Phone and Charger

- **Description:** Even if your cruise ship offers Wi-Fi, the costs can be high (usually $10 to $30 per day). Consider downloading maps and travel apps that work offline, or purchase a local SIM card for better rates while in port.

- **Tip:** Bring a portable charger (about $20) so your phone doesn't run out of battery while exploring.

4. Adapters and Converters

- **Description:** The Baltic region uses a mix of plug types, depending on the country. A universal travel adapter (costing around $15) will allow you to charge your electronics in multiple countries. If you're bringing high-powered devices like hairdryers, check if you need a voltage converter as well.

- Tip: Many cruise ship cabins use U.S. plug types, but always double-check before your trip.

Clothing and Accessories for Formal Nights and Casual Days

Cruise lines typically have dress codes for different parts of the day, so it's important to pack appropriately for both casual days onboard and formal nights in the main dining room.

Casual Days

During the day, the dress code onboard most ships is casual. Here's what to pack:

- Comfortable Clothing: Opt for breathable, comfortable clothes such as t-shirts, shorts, or casual dresses. Brands like Old Navy or Uniqlo offer affordable, comfortable options in the $20 to $40 range.

- Swimwear: Even though the Baltic region may not be tropical, most cruise ships feature heated pools and hot tubs. Don't forget to pack a swimsuit and cover-up, especially if your ship has a spa area.

- Flip Flops or Sandals: Pack a pair of flip flops or sandals (prices range from $10 to $40) for lounging by the pool or strolling around the ship.

Formal Nights

Many Baltic Sea cruises feature one or two formal nights where the dress code is more elegant. Here's how to dress for these occasions:

- **For Men:** Pack a suit or a nice blazer with dress pants. Tuxedos are often optional But can be a fun way to embrace the cruise's glamour. A quality suit from stores like J.Crew or Banana Republic can range from $150 to $400.

- **For Women:** Bring an evening gown, cocktail dress, or formal pantsuit. Retailers like Nordstrom or Macy's offer stylish formal dresses starting around $100.

- **Accessories: Don't** forget to pack formal shoes, a clutch, and any jewelry or accessories to complement your outfit.

What to Leave at Home: Cruise Ship Restrictions

While packing, it's essential to remember that cruise ships have specific restrictions on what you can and cannot bring onboard. Here's what you should leave at home:

1. Irons and Steamers

- **Reason:** Due to fire hazards, most cruise ships prohibit irons, clothes steamers, and other heating devices.

- **Alternative:** Ask your cabin steward for an ironing service, or use the ship's laundry facilities, which typically charge $2 to $5 per item.

2. Power Surge Protectors

- **Reason:** Surge protectors are banned on most ships due to fire safety concerns.

- **Alternative:** Pack a cruise-approved power strip without a surge protector. These typically cost around $15 to $25.

3. Candles and Incense

- **Reason:** Anything with an open flame is strictly prohibited onboard.

- **Alternative:** If you enjoy calming scents, pack a battery-operated diffuser (usually priced around $20 to $40) to freshen your cabin.

4. Large Quantities of Alcohol

- **Reason:** Most cruise lines limit the amount of alcohol you can bring onboard. For example, Royal Caribbean allows one bottle of wine per adult.

- **Tip:** Check your cruise line's alcohol policy in advance to avoid having items confiscated at embarkation.

Chapter 6

Cruising with Family – Fun for All Ages

Cruising the Baltic Sea is a fantastic vacation option for families of all shapes and sizes. With a blend of cultural experiences, breathtaking landscapes, and diverse ports of call, there is something to captivate each member of the family, from toddlers to grandparents. On board the cruise ships, family-friendly amenities ensure that kids, teens, and adults can have an exciting and relaxing time. Whether you're planning for a multigenerational adventure or need to keep the kids entertained while exploring rich historical sites, this chapter will guide you through everything you need to know for a fun-filled family cruise.

Kid-Friendly Features on Baltic Sea Cruises

Cruise lines know how important it is to create an engaging experience for younger travelers. Many ships have kid-specific features designed to entertain and educate children of all ages. These ships provide an endless array of activities and amenities tailored for younger guests, ensuring a memorable vacation for both kids and parents.

Kids' Clubs

Most Baltic Sea cruises offer onboard kids' clubs with structured activities led by trained professionals. These clubs are often divided by age groups, ensuring age-appropriate activities for everyone.

- **Example:** Royal Caribbean's Adventure Ocean program offers separate clubs for kids aged 3 to 5 (Aquanauts), 6 to 8 (Explorers), and 9 to 11 (Voyagers). Activities range from scavenger hunts and arts and crafts to science experiments. The club is free to use and operates during the day and into the evening.

- **Cost:** Free, although some lines may charge for late-night group babysitting (around $7 per hour).

- **Hours:** Open daily, usually from 9:00 AM to midnight.

Splash Pools and Water Slides

Many cruise ships feature water play areas specifically designed for younger kids. These areas are often shallow, making them perfect for splashing around, with colorful slides and fountains to keep the little ones entertained for hours.

- **Example:** Norwegian Cruise Line's Splash Academy and Kids' Aqua Park feature fun water slides and splash zones with colorful characters, catering to kids of all ages.

- **Cost:** Free for all cruise passengers.

- **Website:** http://www.ncl.com

Character Meet-and-Greets

Some cruise lines, like Disney and Royal Caribbean, offer opportunities for kids to meet their favorite characters.

These special meet-and-greets include beloved Disney characters like Mickey and Minnie, as well as DreamWorks favorites such as Shrek and the Penguins of Madagascar.

- **Cost:** Free with your cruise fare.

- **Tip:** Check your daily cruise schedule to know when and where these character appearances will take place to avoid long lines.

Onboard Activities, Family Suites, and Dining Options

When cruising with family, it's important to know that there are numerous activities, spacious accommodations, and flexible dining options to suit everyone's needs.

Onboard Activities for the Entire Family

Cruises offer a plethora of family-friendly activities to enjoy together. From interactive game shows to mini-golf and trivia contests, there's no shortage of things to do.

- **Family Game Shows**: Shows like Family Feud or The Newlywed Game allow families to compete together in a fun, light-hearted competition.

- **Mini-Golf and Rock Climbing:** Ships like Royal Caribbean's Serenade of the Seas have mini-golf courses and rock climbing walls for some family-friendly adventure.

- **Cost:** Free for all passengers.

- **Outdoor Movie Nights:** Many cruise ships feature outdoor movie screens where families can watch popular movies under the stars.

Family Suites

To make your family trip as comfortable as possible, many ships offer spacious family suites that can accommodate larger groups. These suites typically include separate sleeping areas for parents and kids, and some even come with extra amenities like game consoles and private balconies.

- **Example:** Royal Caribbean's Ultimate Family Suite comes with a slide, LEGO wall, air hockey table, and a private movie theater. It's perfect for larger families who want a luxurious experience with plenty of entertainment options.

- **Cost:** Prices for family suites vary greatly depending on the cruise line and season, but expect to pay between $3,000 and $10,000 per week for a suite that accommodates four to six people.

Family Dining Options

One of the highlights of any cruise is the dining experience, and Baltic Sea cruises offer a variety of family-friendly dining options.

- **Main Dining Rooms:** Most cruise lines have main dining rooms that offer kid-friendly menus, high chairs, and booster seats. Family meals are a great time to unwind together after a busy day exploring.

- **Specialty Restaurants:** If you're looking for a special dining experience, consider a specialty restaurant. Many cruise lines have Italian, steakhouse, or sushi restaurants that offer kids' menus, so there's something for everyone.

- **Example**: Celebrity Cruises' Tuscan Grille offers an Italian menu with kid-friendly options like pasta and pizza, with prices for adults starting at $45 per person for a multi-course meal.

- **Website:** http://www.celebritycruises.com

How to Keep Teens and Tweens Entertained

Keeping teens and tweens entertained on a family vacation can be challenging, but cruise lines know how to cater to these age groups with a variety of activities that allow them to explore and socialize on their terms.

Adventure and Gaming

Many ships have state-of-the-art gaming centers, sports complexes, and other activities specifically for teens and tweens.

1. Teen Clubs

- **Description:** Teen clubs are cool hangout spaces where teens can play video games, listen to music, or just relax with new friends. These clubs are often designed to give teens a sense of independence, with supervised activities like dance parties and movie nights.

- **Example:** Norwegian Cruise Line's Entourage teen club, for guests aged 13 to 17, offers video games, movies, and even late-night dance parties.

- **Cost:** Free for all guests.

2. Sports and Adventure

- **Basketball and Soccer Courts:** Teens can join in on pick-up games of basketball or soccer at onboard sports courts.

- **Laser Tag and Escape Rooms**: Some ships, such as Royal Caribbean's Symphony of the Seas, feature laser tag arenas and escape rooms for teens looking for a little extra adventure.

- **Cost:** Laser tag costs around $10 per person, while escape rooms are priced around $20 to $30 per person.

- **Website:** http://www.royalcaribbean.com

3. Arcades and Gaming Lounges

- **Description:** Teens who love video games can head to the arcade or gaming lounges for some fun. With everything from classic pinball machines to the latest video game consoles, these areas are always a hit.

- **Cost:** Some arcades charge per game (usually $1–$2), while others have unlimited game passes available.

Baltic Sea Cruises for Multigenerational Families

Cruises are the perfect vacation for multigenerational families, as they offer something for every age group. Whether you're traveling with young children, teens, parents, or grandparents, the variety of activities, entertainment, and excursions available makes it easy for everyone to have a memorable time.

Choosing the Right Cruise Line

When traveling with multiple generations, it's important to choose a cruise line that caters to everyone's needs. Look for ships with a mix of activities, relaxation options, and excursions that appeal to different age groups.

- **Example:** Holland America Line is known for its more relaxed and cultural experiences, which tend to appeal to older travelers, while still offering kid-friendly activities like Club HAL for children and teens.

- **Cost:** Holland America Line's 7-day Baltic cruises range from $1,200 to $3,500 per person, depending on the cabin and time of year.

- **Website:** http://www.hollandamerica.com

Family-Friendly Excursions

Look for excursions that offer something for everyone in the family. Many Baltic ports of call offer a wide range of excursions, from historical walking tours to outdoor adventures.

- **Example:** In Tallinn, Estonia, take a guided walking tour through the medieval Old Town, followed by a relaxing lunch at a local café. Meanwhile, teens can explore the city walls or climb to the top of St. Olaf's Church for panoramic views.

- **Cost:** Walking tours typically cost around $20 to $50 per person, while admission to St. Olaf's Church costs around $3.

Best Ports and Activities for All Ages

The Baltic Sea is filled with ports that offer family-friendly activities, making it the perfect region for a family cruise. Here are some of the best ports and activities for travelers of all ages:

1. Copenhagen, Denmark

- **Tivoli Gardens:** This classic amusement park is a must-see for families. With rides for both young children and thrill-seeking teens, as well as beautiful gardens and live performances, there's something for everyone.

- **Cost:** Admission is around $20 for adults, with ride tickets sold separately.

- **Tip:** Visit in the evening to enjoy the magical lights and nighttime performances.

- **Website:** http://www.tivoli.dk

2. Stockholm, Sweden

- **Skansen Open-Air Museum:** This family-friendly museum is home to a zoo, historic buildings, and traditional Swedish folk performances, making it a fun and educational experience for all ages.

- **Cost:** Admission is $25 for adults and $8 for children.

- **Website:** http://www.skansen.se

3. Helsinki, Finland

- **Suomenlinna Sea Fortress:** A UNESCO World Heritage site, Suomenlinna is a great spot for families to explore together. Its expansive grounds, tunnels, and fortifications offer plenty of room for kids to run around, while adults can enjoy the history and scenic views.

- **Cost:** Free to explore, with guided tours available for around $10 per person.

- **Website**: http://www.suomenlinna.fi.

Chapter 7

Navigating Health and Safety on Your Cruise

Traveling on a Baltic Sea cruise is an exciting experience, but it's essential to prioritize health and safety to ensure that your journey is smooth and stress-free. From the health services available on board to staying safe while exploring foreign ports, being prepared and informed can make all the difference. This chapter will walk you through everything you need to know about cruise ship health services, onboard medical facilities, how to stay safe at sea and in port, and tips on preventing seasickness. By the end of this guide, you'll be fully equipped to enjoy your cruise with peace of mind.

Cruise Ship Health Services: What You Need to Know

Every major cruise line is equipped with medical services to help passengers deal with illnesses, injuries, or medical emergencies. These services ensure that passengers can access medical care while at sea, but it's important to understand how they work and what costs you might incur.

Onboard Health Clinics

Most cruise ships have a medical facility staffed by qualified doctors and nurses. These clinics are capable of treating common ailments such as colds, minor injuries, and seasickness. However, their capacity for handling major medical emergencies is limited.

- **Services Provided:** Common treatments include administering medications, treating minor injuries like sprains or cuts, and providing care for seasickness or dehydration. More severe medical conditions may require passengers to be evacuated to the nearest port.

- **Cost:** Onboard medical care can be expensive. A visit to the ship's doctor typically costs between $100 and $200, not including additional fees for medications, treatments, or diagnostic tests. Many health insurance plans do not cover medical expenses incurred on a cruise, so purchasing travel insurance is highly recommended (more on that later).

- **Operating Hours:** Most medical centers onboard are open during regular hours (usually from 9:00 AM to 11:00 AM and 3:00 PM to 5:00 PM), but doctors are available 24/7 for emergencies.

Common Health Issues Treated

The most common health problems treated onboard include respiratory infections, gastrointestinal issues, motion sickness, and dehydration. The medical team is equipped to provide basic care for these ailments, including IV fluids for dehydration or anti-nausea medications for seasickness.

Medical Facilities and Onboard Doctors

Cruise ship medical facilities are generally smaller and more limited than a land-based hospital, but they are well-equipped to handle most common medical needs.

What to Expect in a Ship's Medical Facility

The onboard clinic typically includes examination rooms, treatment rooms, and basic diagnostic equipment like EKG machines and X-ray machines. Doctors and nurses are usually trained in emergency medicine and can handle a variety of situations.

- **Staffing:** Ships usually have one or two doctors and several nurses on staff. These medical professionals are licensed and qualified, often with experience in emergency or family medicine.

- **Medical Supplies:** The clinic is stocked with essential medications, bandages, oxygen, and other supplies necessary for emergency care. However, if you need specialized medication or treatment, the clinic may not have it readily available, so it's a good idea to pack any essential medications you use.

- **Cost of Services:** Diagnostic tests, such as blood work or X-rays, can range from $150 to $500 depending on the complexity of the test. Medications, IV fluids, and other treatments will add to the total cost, so it's crucial to be aware of the expenses.

What Happens if You Fall Ill at Sea

While no one likes to think about falling ill on vacation, it's important to be prepared for the possibility. If you do become sick or injured during your cruise, here's what you can expect in terms of care and next steps.

Initial Care Onboard

If you start to feel unwell, the first step is to visit the onboard clinic. If your symptoms are mild, you'll receive treatment right away. However, if you have more serious symptoms, such as chest pain or difficulty breathing, the medical team will evaluate you for further care.

- **Emergency Care:** For severe medical emergencies, such as heart attacks or strokes, the medical staff will stabilize you before deciding whether an emergency evacuation is necessary. Helicopter evacuations or high-speed boat transfers to the nearest hospital are used for life-threatening situations, but these services can cost tens of thousands of dollars.

- **Evacuation to Nearest Port:** If your condition requires more advanced care than what the onboard clinic can provide, the ship's medical team will arrange for you to be disembarked at the nearest port where appropriate medical care is available. This could involve transferring to a local hospital for further treatment.

Staying Safe at Sea and in Port

Cruise ships and ports are generally very safe, but staying vigilant and taking a few extra precautions can ensure your trip remains trouble-free.

Onboard Safety Tips

1. Follow Safety Drills: Upon embarking, cruise lines conduct a mandatory safety drill known as a muster drill. This drill teaches you what to do in case of an emergency, where your lifeboat is located, and how to use a life vest. Pay close attention to these drills—they could save your life in the event of an emergency.

2. Keep Valuables in the Safe: Cruise cabins are equipped with a personal safe for storing passports, jewelry, and other valuable items. Always use this safe to minimize the risk of theft.

3. Be Careful on Wet Decks: Slip-and-fall injuries are one of the most common accidents on cruise ships. Watch for wet decks near pools or outdoor areas and wear non-slip shoes to reduce your risk.

Port Safety Tips

Exploring new cities and countries is one of the best parts of a Baltic cruise, but it's important to remain aware of your surroundings and follow local safety guidelines.

1. Travel in Groups: It's always safer to explore port cities in a group, especially in crowded areas or tourist-heavy attractions. Stick to well-lit and well-traveled areas.

2. Watch for Pickpockets: Popular tourist destinations like Nyhavn in Copenhagen or Old Town in Tallinn can attract pickpockets. Keep your belongings close and consider using an anti-theft backpack or money belt.

3. Stay Hydrated and Rested: Exploring port cities can be physically demanding. Make sure to stay hydrated and take breaks when needed, especially in warmer weather.

Security Tips for Baltic Sea Cruises

The Baltic region is known for its safety, but following basic security measures ensures your trip is as smooth as possible.

- Avoid Flashing Valuables: Wearing expensive jewelry or flashing large amounts of cash can attract unwanted attention. Keep valuables discreet and use credit cards or travel cards instead of carrying large amounts of cash.

- Secure Your Luggage: If you plan on leaving your bags in your cabin, make sure your luggage is locked. If you're leaving items in a public area on board (like pool decks or lounges), keep an eye on your belongings or ask a family member to stay with them.

- Check Travel Advisories: Before you head to port, check the latest travel advisories or consult your cruise line's safety briefing. Some areas may have specific warnings or restrictions that you'll need to know about.

Travel Insurance: Why You Need It and How to Get It

One of the most important aspects of preparing for your cruise is securing comprehensive travel insurance. A well-rounded policy can cover unexpected medical expenses, trip cancellations, or lost luggage.

Why You Need Travel Insurance

1. Medical Expenses: As previously mentioned, onboard medical services are expensive, and your regular health insurance may not cover you outside of your home country. Travel insurance can cover these costs, including emergency medical evacuation.

2. Trip Cancellations: Travel insurance can reimburse you for non-refundable expenses if your trip is canceled due to illness, family emergencies, or unforeseen circumstances like natural disasters.

3. Lost Luggage: If your luggage is lost or delayed, insurance can help cover the cost of replacing essential items such as clothing, medications, and toiletries.

How to Get Travel Insurance

Several reputable providers specialize in cruise travel insurance, including:

- **Allianz Travel Insurance:** Offers comprehensive plans that cover medical emergencies, trip cancellations, and lost luggage. Plans range from $150 to $300 depending on the length and cost of your cruise.

- Travel Guard: Known for their customizable policies, Travel Guard provides coverage tailored to cruising, including medical evacuation and missed port coverage.

- Website: http://www.allianztravelinsurance.com

www.travelguard.com](http://www.travelguard.com

Seasickness Prevention and Treatment

Even seasoned travelers can experience seasickness, particularly on open-water routes like the Baltic Sea. Fortunately, there are many ways to prevent and treat motion sickness.

Prevention Tips

1. Choose the Right Cabin: If you're prone to seasickness, book a cabin on a lower deck in the middle of the ship, where the motion of the boat is less noticeable.

2. Wear Motion Sickness Bands: Acupressure wristbands, such as Sea-Bands ($10 to $15), apply pressure to a specific point on the wrist and can help reduce nausea.

3. Take Medication: Over-the-counter medications like Dramamine ($10) or Bonine ($8) are effective in preventing and treating seasickness. These should be taken before symptoms begin.

4. Stay Hydrated and Eat Lightly: Drink plenty of water and avoid heavy, greasy foods, which can exacerbate nausea.

Onboard Treatments

If you do start to feel unwell while at sea, the ship's medical center can provide motion sickness Injections or stronger anti-nausea medications for immediate relief. These services typically cost around $50 to $100.

By planning and being mindful of these health and safety tips, you'll be well-prepared for any situation that may arise on your Baltic Sea cruise. Whether you're enjoying the onboard facilities or exploring port cities, a little preparation can go a long way toward ensuring a safe and enjoyable vacation.

Chapter 8

Sustainable Cruising in the Baltic Sea

In recent years, the demand for eco-friendly travel has surged, and cruising is no exception. As more travelers seek to reduce their environmental footprint, cruise lines are responding by adopting sustainable practices and implementing measures to protect the delicate ecosystems of the regions they visit, including the pristine waters of the Baltic Sea. Whether you're an eco-conscious traveler or simply want to minimize your environmental impact, this chapter will provide you with insight into how to cruise more sustainably in the Baltic Sea and beyond. From choosing a green cruise line to supporting local economies through responsible shore excursions, there are many ways to contribute to sustainable travel.

Eco-Friendly Cruise Lines: Choosing a Green Cruise

One of the first steps toward cruising sustainably is selecting an eco-friendly cruise line. Many cruise companies are making significant strides toward reducing their environmental impact, from cutting emissions to minimizing waste. When booking your Baltic Sea cruise, consider a company that prioritizes environmental responsibility.

Cruise Lines Leading the Green Movement

1. Hurtigruten

- **Description:** Hurtigruten is considered a pioneer in sustainable cruising. Known for its eco-friendly expedition ships, Hurtigruten is committed to operating with a minimal environmental footprint. The company uses hybrid electric-powered ships to reduce emissions and sources locally produced, sustainable food for its onboard restaurants.

- **Sustainable Practices:** Hybrid propulsion systems, reduced plastic use, and no single-use plastics onboard.

- **Average Cost**: Hurtigruten cruises are typically more expensive than standard cruises, with 7-day Baltic itineraries starting at around $2,000 per person.

- **Website:** http://www.hurtigruten.com

2. MSC Cruises

- **Description:** MSC Cruises has made significant progress toward becoming a more sustainable cruise line by investing in cutting-edge technology to improve energy efficiency and reduce waste. MSC's ships feature advanced wastewater treatment systems and energy-saving technologies like LED lighting and energy recovery systems.

- Sustainable Practices: Advanced wastewater treatment, energy efficiency measures, and reducing CO_2 emissions.

- Average Cost: MSC Cruises offers more affordable options, with Baltic itineraries starting at $1,000 to $1,500 per person for a 7-day cruise.

- Website: http://www.msccruises.com

What to Look for in a Sustainable Cruise Line

When researching cruise lines, look for those that meet the following environmental standards:

- Waste Management: Does the cruise line have a strategy for minimizing and recycling waste onboard?

- Energy Efficiency: Do the ships use energy-saving technologies such as hybrid engines or solar power?

- Environmental Certifications: Look for companies certified by recognized environmental organizations such as Green Marine or the Global Sustainable Tourism Council (GSTC).

How Cruise Companies Are Addressing Environmental Impact

Cruise companies are under increasing pressure to reduce their environmental footprint, and many are stepping up to the challenge. From cleaner fuel options to waste management, here's how the cruise industry is tackling its environmental impact.

Cleaner Fuels and Emissions Reductions

One of the primary ways cruise lines are working to lower their environmental impact is by switching to cleaner fuel sources. Ships traditionally relied on heavy fuel oil, which is highly polluting. Now, many lines are transitioning to liquefied natural gas (LNG) and adopting emissions-reducing technology.

- **Example:** Costa Cruises has introduced LNG-powered ships that significantly reduce CO2 and sulfur emissions. Ships like Costa Smeralda run on LNG, reducing greenhouse gas emissions by up to 25%.

- **Cost:** LNG ships are generally more expensive to operate, but these costs are often offset by the growing demand for sustainable travel, with prices similar to other high-end cruises (from $2,500 per person for a 7-day itinerary).

Waste Management and Recycling

Reducing waste is another key focus for sustainable cruising. Many cruise lines now have sophisticated recycling and waste management systems onboard. Ships are increasingly equipped to treat and purify wastewater before it is discharged, and some lines are even recycling food waste to reduce their carbon footprint.

- **Example:** Royal Caribbean has invested heavily in state-of-the-art waste treatment facilities that recycle almost all of the waste generated onboard, and the company is actively working to eliminate single-use plastics.

- Cost: These initiatives add little to the cost of your cruise fare but offer significant environmental benefits.

Reducing Your Carbon Footprint on a Cruise

While cruise ships work to reduce their environmental impact, there are several steps you can take to minimize your carbon footprint while cruising the Baltic Sea.

Choose an Eco-Friendly Cabin

Consider booking an inside cabin, which requires less energy to heat and cool compared to balcony cabins. Inside cabins often cost significantly less than balcony cabins, with savings ranging from $500 to $1,000 depending on the cruise line and season.

Minimize Water and Energy Use

Be mindful of your water and energy consumption while onboard. Simple actions like reusing towels, turning off lights when leaving your cabin, and taking shorter showers can make a big difference.

- Tip: Many cruise ships now have energy-efficient lighting and water-saving showerheads, but passengers can still help by reducing wasteful habits.

Offset Your Carbon Emissions

Many cruise lines offer passengers the option to purchase carbon offsets, which help to neutralize the emissions generated during their trip. The cost of these offsets can range from $10 to $50 per person, depending on the length and carbon intensity of the cruise.

- **Example:** Norwegian Cruise Line offers a carbon offset program where passengers can purchase credits that support renewable energy projects worldwide.

- **Website:** http://www.ncl.com

Simple Ways to Cruise More Sustainably

In addition to choosing a sustainable cruise line, there are many small steps you can take to cruise more sustainably. These simple actions can have a big impact on reducing waste, conserving resources, and supporting the environment.

Bring a Reusable Water Bottle

Many cruise ships now have water refill stations, making it easy to bring a reusable water bottle and avoid buying plastic bottles. Not only does this reduce waste, but it also saves money.

- **Cost:** Reusable water bottles cost between $15 and $40, depending on the brand and material (stainless steel options tend to be more durable and eco-friendly).

Pack Eco-Friendly Toiletries

Opt for biodegradable shampoos, soaps, and sunscreens to minimize harmful chemicals being washed into the ocean. Many cruise lines, including MSC Cruises, now recommend that passengers use reef-safe sunscreens to protect marine life.

- **Cost**: Eco-friendly toiletries like reef-safe sunscreen typically range from $10 to $25.

- **Tip:** Check with your cruise line to see if they provide eco-friendly toiletries in the cabins, which can save you packing space.

Limit Plastic Use

Bring your reusable shopping bags and refuse single-use plastics where possible. Many ports are making efforts to reduce plastic waste, and travelers can contribute by bringing their bags or containers when shopping or dining.

Supporting Local Economies: Responsible Shore Excursions

When visiting the beautiful cities and towns along the Baltic Sea, consider choosing shore excursions that benefit local economies and promote sustainable tourism. By booking tours with locally-owned operators, purchasing goods from local artisans, and engaging in eco-friendly activities, you can help support the communities you visit.

Eco-Friendly Shore Excursions

Many ports now offer eco-conscious shore excursions that allow you to explore the destination sustainably. Whether it's a walking tour, a bike tour, or a visit to a local farm, these tours are designed to minimize environmental impact while providing an authentic experience.

- **Example:** In Helsinki, Finland, you can join a guided bike tour of the city's green spaces and historical sites. These tours cost around $50 to $75 per person and offer an environmentally friendly way to explore Helsinki.

- **Website:** http://www.myhelsinki.fi

Buy Local, Support Artisans

Purchasing locally-made products rather than mass-produced souvenirs is an excellent way to support the local economy. Whether it's hand-woven textiles in Estonia or handcrafted jewelry in Latvia, these purchases have a direct positive impact on the communities you visit.

- **Cost:** Prices vary, but you can expect to pay between $20 and $100 for high-quality local goods.

Take Part in Cultural Experiences

Supporting cultural tours or workshops that preserve local traditions is another great way to travel responsibly. Consider taking part in a cooking class or folk craft workshop, where you'll learn from local experts while also contributing to the preservation of their traditions.

- **Example:** In Tallinn, Estonia, you can participate in a traditional Estonian handicraft workshop, learning how to make leather goods or knit woolen garments. These workshops range from $30 to $60 per person and offer a hands-on experience in local craftsmanship.

- **Website:** http://www.visittallinn.ee

Chapter 9

Budgeting for Your Baltic Sea Cruise

Planning a Baltic Sea cruise involves more than just choosing a cruise line and selecting your favorite ports of call—it also requires careful budgeting to ensure that you enjoy your vacation without breaking the bank. From understanding the costs of different cabin choices and shore excursions to managing gratuities and currency exchange in various Baltic countries, this chapter will guide you through everything you need to know to effectively budget for your Baltic Sea adventure. With practical money-saving tips, advice on when and how to book, and strategies for handling payments while in port, you'll be able to cruise comfortably while keeping your expenses in check.

Cruise Costs Breakdown: What to Expect

When planning your Baltic Sea cruise, it's crucial to have a clear understanding of the different costs involved. Cruise fares typically cover basic accommodations, meals in main dining venues, and onboard entertainment, but several additional costs can quickly add up if you're not careful.

1. Cruise Fare

The cost of your cruise fare will depend on several factors, including the cruise line, cabin type, and time of year. For example:

- **Average Cruise Fare:** Expect to pay between $1,200 and $2,500 per person for a 7-day Baltic Sea cruise. This price usually includes your cabin, meals in the main dining areas, and most onboard activities.

- **Example:** A mid-range balcony cabin on a cruise with MSC Cruises typically starts at around $1,500 per person, while a suite on a more luxurious line like Celebrity Cruises could cost upwards of $3,000 per person for the same duration.

2. Cabin Choices and Costs

Choosing the right cabin is one of the most significant decisions you'll make when budgeting for your cruise. Cabins range from budget-friendly inside staterooms to opulent suites, and the cost difference can be significant.

- **Inside Cabins:** These are the most affordable option, typically costing between $1,000 and $1,500 per person for a 7-day cruise.

- **Oceanview Cabins:** Offering a view of the sea, these cabins range from $1,300 to $1,800 per person.

- **Balcony Cabins:** For those who want a private outdoor space, balcony cabins cost between $1,500 and $2,500 per person.

- **Suites:** Luxury suites come with additional perks like priority boarding, but they can cost anywhere from $3,000 to $6,000 per person, depending on the cruise line and season.

Cabin Choices, Shore Excursions, Gratuities, and Specialty Dining

Once you've chosen your cabin, you'll need to consider several other expenses that can add to the overall cost of your Baltic cruise.

1. Shore Excursions

Shore excursions are one of the most exciting parts of a Baltic Sea cruise, but they can also be a significant additional expense. Whether you choose guided tours or independent exploration, the costs can vary greatly.

- **Guided Shore Excursions:** Cruise lines offer a range of guided shore excursions that cover everything from city tours to outdoor adventures. Prices typically range from $50 to $200 per person, depending on the activity.

- **Example:** A guided tour of St. Petersburg, Russia, which includes visits to the Hermitage Museum and Peterhof Palace, could cost around $150 per person.

- **DIY Shore Excursions:** For budget-conscious travelers, exploring ports independently can save you money. You can take public transport, rent bikes, or simply walk around. In cities like Tallinn, Estonia, and Copenhagen, Denmark, public transportation is reliable and affordable. A day pass for Copenhagen's public transport costs around $12 per person.

2. Gratuities

Gratuities are often an additional charge on top of your cruise fare, and they're typically added automatically to your onboard account.

- **Average Gratuity Costs**: Most cruise lines charge around $14 to $18 per person, per day for gratuities. This covers the service provided by your cabin steward, dining staff, and other crew members. For a 7-day cruise, gratuities can total between $100 and $130 per person.

- **Example: On** Royal Caribbean, gratuities are $16 per person, per day for standard cabins and $18.50 per person, per day for suites.

3. Specialty Dining

While meals in the main dining rooms and buffets are included in your fare, specialty restaurants often come with an additional charge.

- **Specialty Restaurant Costs:** Depending on the restaurant, dining fees range from $25 to $60 per person. Popular specialty restaurants include steakhouses, sushi bars, and Italian trattorias.

- **Example:** Celebrity Cruises' Murano French restaurant charges about $50 per person for a multi-course meal, while Norwegian Cruise Line's Cagney's Steakhouse costs around $45 per person.

Money-Saving Tips for Baltic Sea Cruises

While cruising the Baltic can be pricey, there are plenty of ways to save money and stay within your budget. Here are some tips to keep your cruise costs manageable.

1. Book Early or Last Minute

Booking early often gets you the best prices and cabin choices, but last-minute deals can also save you money if you're flexible with your dates and itinerary.

- **Early Booking:** Cruise lines frequently offer early-bird discounts of 10% to 20% off the standard fare if you book six months to a year in advance.

- **Last-Minute Deals:** If you're able to book at the last minute (within 60 to 90 days of departure), you can often find significant discounts on unsold cabins.

2. Look for All-Inclusive Packages

Some cruise lines offer all-inclusive packages that include drinks, Wi-Fi, and gratuities. While these packages cost more upfront, they can save you money in the long run by eliminating unexpected onboard expenses.

- **Example:** MSC Cruises' All-Inclusive Easy Drinks Package starts at $35 per day and includes unlimited beverages such as cocktails, wine, beer, and soft drinks. Over a 7-day cruise, this could save you hundreds of dollars compared to paying for drinks individually.

3. Travel During Shoulder Season

Cruising during the shoulder season (May or September) can save you money compared to peak summer months. Not only are cruise fares lower, but ports are less crowded, and you may find cheaper flights and hotels.

- **Cost Savings:** Shoulder season cruise fares can be 20% to 30% cheaper than summer fares. For instance, a 7-day cruise in June might cost $2,000 per person, while the same cruise in September could be as low as $1,500.

When to Book, How to Find Deals, and Saving on Extras

When searching for the greatest cruise discounts, timing is everything. Here's how to make sure you're getting the most value for your money.

1. When to Book

- **Best Time to Book:** The ideal time to book a cruise is during the cruise line's annual sales events, such as Black Friday, Wave Season (January to March), and their mid-year sales. These periods often offer the lowest fares and extra perks like onboard credits or free upgrades.

- **Cancellation Policies:** Many cruise lines allow free cancellations up to a certain date before departure, which can give you flexibility if a better deal comes along after you book.

2. How to Find Deals

- **Cruise Booking Websites:** Websites like CruiseCritic, VacationsToGo, and Expedia frequently list discounted cruises, flash sales, and last-minute deals. You can also sign up for price alerts to get notified when prices drop on cruises you're interested in.

- **Example:** VacationsToGo often advertises Baltic cruises with up to 60% off standard fares.

3. Saving on Extras

Extras like drinks, Wi-Fi, and spa treatments can quickly add up. Consider purchasing packages in advance to save money.

- **Wi-Fi Packages:** Purchasing a Wi-Fi package before your cruise can save you up to 20% compared to onboard prices. Prices typically range from $10 to $25 per day, depending on the package.

- **Drink Packages:** If you enjoy cocktails or specialty coffee, a drink package can offer significant savings. Onboard, individual drinks usually cost $8 to $15, while a drink package typically costs around $50 to $70 per day and includes unlimited drinks.

Currency and Payments in Baltic Countries

Each Baltic port you visit will likely use a different currency, so it's important to know how to handle payments and manage currency exchanges while traveling.

1. Common Currencies in the Baltic Region

- **Denmark:** Danish Krone (DKK)

- **Sweden:** Swedish Krona (SEK)

- **Finland,** Estonia, Latvia, and Germany: Euro (EUR)

- **Russia:** Russian Ruble (RUB)

2. Using Credit Cards

Credit and debit cards are widely accepted in most Baltic countries, especially in tourist areas, but it's always a good idea to have some local currency on hand for small purchases, public transport, or local markets.

- **Tip:** Use a credit card that doesn't charge foreign transaction fees, as these fees can add up throughout your trip. Popular options include the Chase Sapphire Preferred or the Capital One Venture card, both of which offer no foreign transaction fees and travel rewards.

What to Know About Handling Money in Port

When exploring Baltic cities, you'll want to be aware of currency exchange rates, ATM fees, and the best ways to handle your money while in port.

1. Exchanging Currency

While it's convenient to exchange some currency before your cruise, you'll often find better exchange rates at ATMs in the Baltic countries. However, be mindful of any fees that your bank may charge for international ATM withdrawals.

- **Tip:** Check whether your bank has partnerships with foreign banks to avoid additional ATM fees. For example, Bank of America partners with Deutsche Bank in Germany, allowing for fee-free withdrawals.

2. Using Local ATMs

ATMs are readily available in Baltic ports and offer the best exchange rates. However, some ATMs may charge a withdrawal fee, typically ranging from $3 to $5 per transaction.

- **Tip:** Always choose to be charged in the local currency (not USD) at ATMs and payment terminals to avoid hidden conversion fees.

3. Safety Tips for Handling Money

When withdrawing cash or making payments in port, be mindful of your surroundings and take basic precautions.

- **Use a Money Belt:** If you're carrying large amounts of cash or important documents like your passport, consider wearing a money belt to keep your belongings secure.

- Notify Your Bank: Before traveling, notify your bank of your travel plans to avoid having your card blocked for suspected fraud.

Chapter 10

Baltic Sea Cruise FAQs

When preparing for your first Baltic Sea cruise, you're likely to have many questions—ranging from logistical concerns to what to expect during your trip. This chapter is designed to address the most common queries that first-time cruisers have, from visa requirements for St. Petersburg to troubleshooting issues such as lost luggage or medical emergencies. By the end, you'll be equipped with the information you need to ensure a smooth and enjoyable experience on your Baltic cruise.

Common Questions First-Time Cruisers Ask

If you've never been on a cruise before, it's normal to have a lot of questions. Here are some of the most common inquiries first-time cruisers have about their Baltic Sea adventure:

1. What Should I Pack for a Baltic Sea Cruise?

Packing for a Baltic cruise involves preparing for variable weather. Bring a mix of light layers, waterproof jackets, comfortable walking shoes, and formalwear for evening events. Refer to Chapter 5: Baltic Sea Cruise Packing List for a comprehensive guide on what to bring.

2. How Do Shore Excursions Work?

Shore excursions are organized activities that take place at various ports along the cruise route. These can include guided tours, cultural experiences, or outdoor adventures.

You can book excursions through your cruise line or explore independently (see Chapter 4: Shore Excursions for more details).

3. Can I use my cell phone on board the ship?

Yes, you can use your cell phone onboard, but be aware of roaming charges. Most cruise lines offer Wi-Fi packages, which can range from $10 to $25 per day, allowing you to stay connected without incurring hefty phone bills. Check with your mobile provider to see if they offer any cruise-specific data plans.

Do I Need a Visa for St. Petersburg?

Visiting St. Petersburg, Russia is a highlight of many Baltic Sea cruises, but it comes with unique visa requirements that travelers should be aware of.

1. Cruise Line Organized Shore Excursions

If you book a shore excursion through your cruise line, you typically do not need a Russian visa. Cruise lines work with local tour operators who provide blanket visa coverage for passengers participating in official shore excursions. This means you can visit St. Petersburg for up to 72 hours without obtaining an individual visa.

- Example: A guided tour of the Hermitage Museum and Peterhof Palace booked through your cruise line costs around $150 to $200 per person and covers visa requirements.

2. Exploring Independently

If you plan to explore St. Petersburg independently (without booking a cruise line-organized excursion), you will need to apply for a Russian tourist visa in advance. The process can be time-consuming, requiring an invitation letter from a hotel or tour company and an in-person application at a Russian consulate. Visa fees typically range from $80 to $160 depending on your nationality.

- **Tip:** Most travelers opt for the ease of booking an excursion through the cruise line to avoid the visa application process.

3. Using a Private Tour Operator

Some private tour operators in St. Petersburg also offer visa-free tours. They provide the necessary visa documentation as long as you stay with their group for the entire duration of the excursion.

- **Website:** http://www.visitrussia.org.uk

Is Wi-Fi Available on Board?

Yes, Wi-Fi is available on most cruise ships, but the quality and price can vary significantly.

Wi-Fi Costs

Wi-Fi packages on Baltic Sea cruises are usually available for purchase and are priced according to data usage or duration. Prices typically range from $10 to $30 per day, depending on the cruise line and the package you select.

- **Basic Plans:** These typically cover basic internet usage, such as checking emails or social media. These plans range from $10 to $15 per day.

- **Premium Plans:** If you need to stream video, make video calls, or use more bandwidth, expect to pay between $20 and $30 per day for a premium Wi-Fi package.

Wi-Fi Availability

Keep in mind that Wi-Fi connectivity can be spotty when the ship is sailing in remote areas or far from land. Many cruise lines offer designated internet cafés or public Wi-Fi spots onboard.

- **Tip:** To save money, purchase a Wi-Fi package in advance or look for bundles that include Wi-Fi, drink packages, and specialty dining.

What If My Cruise is Canceled or Delayed?

While cruise cancellations or delays are rare, they can happen due to weather conditions, mechanical issues, or other unforeseen circumstances. Here's what you should know in case your cruise is affected.

1. Cancellations

If your cruise is canceled by the cruise line, you will typically receive a full refund or the option to rebook on a future sailing. Some cruise lines may also offer additional compensation in the form of onboard credits or free excursions for future cruises.

- **Example**: Royal Caribbean offers a full refund or rebooking option in the event of a canceled cruise, along with a $300 onboard credit for your next cruise.

2. Delays

In the event of a delay, whether it's due to weather or a technical issue, the cruise line will typically offer compensation such as onboard credits, free meals, or additional amenities during the delay. If a delay affects your flights, the cruise line may assist in rebooking your travel.

- **Tip:** Travel insurance can help cover any non-refundable expenses such as flights or hotels in case of a delay or cancellation (see Chapter 7: Navigating Health and Safety on Your Cruise for more on travel insurance).

Even with careful planning, unexpected issues can arise during your cruise. Here's how to handle common problems that may occur during your Baltic Sea cruise.

1. Lost Luggage

If your luggage is lost or delayed at embarkation, report it immediately to the cruise line's customer service desk. Most cruise lines offer a lost luggage service and will work to track and return your luggage to you at the next port.

- **Tip:** Pack essential items (such as medications and a change of clothes) in your carry-on in case your luggage is delayed.

2. Missed Ports

Occasionally, a port of call may be missed due to weather or other factors. If this happens, the cruise line will usually substitute another port or offer compensation such as onboard credits or a refund for pre-booked shore excursions.

- **Example:** Norwegian Cruise Line offers onboard credits if a port is missed, and passengers are refunded for any shore excursions that were pre-booked for the missed destination.

3. Medical Emergencies

In the event of a medical emergency, the ship's onboard medical staff will provide immediate care. If the situation is serious and requires treatment beyond the ship's capabilities, the passenger may be disembarked at the nearest port and transferred to a local hospital.

- **Cost:** Medical services onboard can be expensive, with consultation fees ranging from $100 to $300 depending on the severity of the issue. Medical evacuation can cost tens of thousands of dollars, so it's vital to have travel insurance that covers medical emergencies.

Lost Luggage, Missed Ports, and Medical Emergencies

Cruising comes with its share of potential hiccups, from misplaced luggage to unexpected medical needs. Here's how to get through these situations smoothly:

1. Handling Lost Luggage

- **Action:** Report your lost luggage immediately to guest services. Cruise lines often work with local authorities and airlines to expedite the delivery of lost items at the next port. Some cruise lines also provide complimentary toiletries and essential clothing items while waiting for your luggage.

2. Missed Ports

- **Action:** If a port is missed due to weather or other uncontrollable factors, the cruise line will often offer compensation, either by refunding pre-booked excursions or by adding onboard credits to your account.

3. Medical Emergencies

- **Action:** Ensure that you have adequate travel insurance that covers medical care and emergency evacuation. If a medical emergency arises, seek immediate assistance from the ship's medical center. In serious cases, arrangements may be made to disembark at the nearest port for hospital treatment.

Final Thoughts

Taking a Baltic Sea cruise is an unforgettable experience, but as with any major trip, being prepared for common issues is key to ensuring everything goes smoothly. By understanding visa requirements, handling onboard logistics like Wi-Fi and gratuities, and knowing how to respond to problems such as missed ports or medical emergencies, you can focus on enjoying the rich history, culture, and beauty of the Baltic region without unnecessary worry.

Conclusion: Your Baltic Sea Adventure Awaits

As you prepare to embark on your Baltic Sea cruise, you are about to enter a world of rich history, breathtaking natural beauty, and diverse cultures that have shaped this fascinating region for centuries. From the medieval charm of Tallinn's Old Town to the imperial grandeur of St. Petersburg, and from the stunning archipelagos of Stockholm to the vibrant art nouveau architecture of Riga, a Baltic cruise offers a once-in-a-lifetime journey that will awaken your senses and expand your horizons.

A cruise is not just about seeing new places; it's about creating lasting memories, forging connections with different cultures, and experiencing the world in ways that simply aren't possible with other forms of travel. Whether you are soaking in the serenity of a quiet fjord, marveling at world-renowned works of art, or tasting local delicacies at a bustling market, The Baltic Sea offers something for everyone, regardless of interests or inclinations.

As you've discovered in this guide, a Baltic Sea cruise offers much more than just scenic views and historic landmarks. It's an immersive experience that weaves together the rich tapestry of history, culture, and modern life across Northern Europe and Russia. From Copenhagen's canals to the pristine forests of Helsinki, each destination brings a unique flavor and experience that will leave you with a deeper appreciation for this part of the world.

The Power of Exploration

Exploring the Baltic Sea is about more than just ticking off destinations from a checklist—it's about truly immersing yourself in the cultures, traditions, and stories that make each port special. As you step off the ship and into cities like Stockholm, Helsinki, and Klaipėda, you'll find that each place offers its distinct blend of ancient history and modern innovation. The cobblestone streets, vibrant markets, and iconic landmarks are all waiting to be explored, inviting you to engage with the people, food, and customs that define them.

As you journey from port to port, you'll notice how interconnected these nations are, yet how each one has maintained its own unique identity. The shared history of trade, politics, and cultural exchange has shaped the Baltic Sea region, and you'll see evidence of this in the architecture, art, and even the cuisine you encounter. From the colorful townhouses of Nyhavn in Copenhagen to the grand palaces of St. Petersburg, the Baltic Sea region is a visual and cultural feast.

And it's not just the destinations themselves that make a Baltic cruise special. The journey itself, sailing through the cold, crisp waters of the northern seas, offers its magic. The wide-open skies, the sound of the ship cutting through the waves, and the ever-changing seascape create a sense of freedom and adventure that's hard to match. Whether you're enjoying a cup of coffee on your balcony or watching the sun dip below the horizon from the deck, The tranquility and beauty of the Baltic Sea will linger with you long after your trip is over.

Creating Lasting Memories

Each port you visit will undoubtedly leave you with its own set of memories, but the onboard experience is equally important in making your trip unforgettable. From the moment you board the ship to the last evening of your cruise, you'll be treated to first-class hospitality, gourmet meals, and entertainment options that range from Broadway-style shows to cooking classes and cultural lectures.

Perhaps you'll meet fellow travelers who share your passion for exploration and adventure. Cruises have a unique way of bringing people together, and you might find yourself forming lasting friendships with other guests who, like you, are there to experience the magic of the Baltic Sea.

In addition to the luxurious onboard amenities, remember to take full advantage of the resources provided by your cruise line, from expert-led excursions to onboard cultural activities. By immersing yourself in the stories and traditions of the region, you'll come away from your cruise not only with great memories but with a deeper understanding of the places you've visited.

A Responsible Approach to Travel

In an era where sustainable travel is becoming increasingly important, a Baltic Sea cruise offers you the opportunity to experience one of the world's most stunning regions while being mindful of your environmental impact. As outlined in Chapter 8: Sustainable Cruising in the Baltic Sea, many cruise lines are adopting greener practices, and you too can contribute by making responsible choices during your trip. Supporting local economies by purchasing locally made goods, participating in eco-friendly excursions, and minimizing your use of single-use plastics onboard are just a few ways you can make a positive impact during your journey.

As you explore this environmentally sensitive region, it's essential to recognize the role we all play in protecting the destinations we visit. The Baltic Sea's natural beauty, from its serene coastlines to its vast archipelagos, is worth preserving for future generations. By choosing to travel responsibly, you are contributing to the long-term sustainability of the region.

A Journey Like No Other

As your cruise draws to a close, and you reflect on the sights, sounds, and experiences that have shaped your journey, you'll likely find that the Baltic Sea has left an indelible mark on you. Whether it's the awe-inspiring grandeur of the Hermitage in St. Petersburg, the tranquil beauty of Helsinki's forests and islands, or the charming medieval streets of Tallinn, each destination tells a story, and together they create a narrative that is as rich as the sea itself.

In the end, a Baltic Sea cruise is more than just a vacation—it's a transformative experience. It's about discovery, connection, and reflection. It's about stepping out of your comfort zone and engaging with new cultures, new ideas, and new landscapes. And it's about taking the time to appreciate the beauty of the world around you, both on land and at sea.

As you disembark and begin your journey home, you'll carry the memories of your Baltic cruise with you—memories that will inspire you to continue exploring, learning, and seeking out new adventures. The world is vast, and the Baltic Sea is just one of its many wonders, but for those who have had the privilege of cruising its waters, it's an experience that will be cherished forever.

So, pack your bags, set sail, and let the Baltic Sea reveal its secrets. Your adventure awaits.

Printed in Dunstable, United Kingdom